The Book of
New Israeli Food
a culinary journey

To my parents, Ada and Ilya Gerzbach,
who taught me everything

A cataloging-in-publication record has been established for this book
by the Library of Congress.

All recipes are kosher.

ISBN 978-0-8052-1224-2

www.schocken.com

Editor: Frances Zetland
Design: Varda Amir
Production: Iris Gelbart

Additional photography:
Daniel Layla: 17 (bottom), 143, 145, 147, 170, 192, 259
Michal Revivo: 15, 151, 222
Danya Weiner: 157, 233, 235, 249, 252, 262, 270, 273
Michal Lehnart: 34, 40, 78, 121, 124, 149, 253
Ilit Azulai: 30
Ronen Mangan: 83
Liat Paz: 257
Yael Ilan: 26 (from "Orna & Ella Cookbook", published by "Ahuzat Bayit")

Printed in China
First American Edition
9 8 7 6 5 4 3 2 1

The author wishes to thank the following people for their invaluable
help in researching and producing this book:
Tova Dickshtein, Shir Halpern, Lilach Rubin, Shmuel Holland, the Safadi
Family (Nazareth), the Karpol Family (Herut), Yael Shavit.

Janna Gur

The Book of New Israeli Food
a culinary journey

Photography
Eilon Paz

Contributing Writers
Rami Hann, Orly Pely-Bronshtein
Adam Montefiore, Ruth Oliver

Schocken Books, New York

Contents

Stories

What's cooking in the melting pot?

They say nobody comes to Israel for the food. There are so many reasons to visit this unique land, food is certainly not at the top of the list. Twenty to thirty years ago the only memorable culinary experiences tourists might have had was a good hummus in the Old City of Jerusalem or a hearty Israeli breakfast at a hotel. If they come back today they're in for a big surprise.

They can savor world-class wines, sip a perfect cup of cappuccino at a seaside café, nibble delectable goat cheeses at a dairy farm in the Galilee, and sample authentic and varied street food. They can wander through open-air markets brimming with fresh produce and exotic goods by day and hang out at trendy bars by night. They can buy almost any conceivable ingredient anywhere in the country, find a vast array of Hebrew language cookbooks in the bookstores, and have a choice of food shows and cooking classes given by professional chefs and amateur food and wine aficionados. Above all, they will discover a vibrant sophisticated restaurant scene where young, internationally trained chefs fuse classic cooking techniques with those of the Middle East. Working

with local ingredients, they embellish their menus with dishes adapted from their family heritage, be it Moroccan, Persian, Hungarian or Turkish.

In less than thirty years Israeli society has graduated from Spartan austerity to a true gastronomic haven.

The Roots

Israel is a young state but its roots go back thousands of years. The first place to look for the origins of local food culture is the Bible. Right from the outset, in Genesis, the Bible is brimming with food, used for welcoming friends and appeasing enemies, for seduction and bribery, for comfort and religious rituals. Food (or the lack of it) often played a pivotal role in Jewish history, such as when famine in Canaan drove the Hebrews down to Egypt.

But what exactly was this food? What was the red stew for which Esau sold his birthright to Jacob? What were the mysterious flagons that Shulamite, beloved of King Solomon, craved in the Song of Songs? What was the magical manna that sustained the Hebrews in the desert? Scientific research has few definite answers and plenty of suppositions.

There was a clear distinction in ancient Israel between two rival societies: shepherds and farmers. The former were nomads who roved the desert with their herds, the latter were permanent dwellers in the mountains and valleys and on the plains. The first hint of their age-old animosity was recorded in the story of Cain (the shepherd) and Abel (the farmer).

Ancient Palestine was a harsh place to grow food, with poor soil and unpredictable rainfall that often resulted in drought and famine. Meat, especially prevalent in shepherd tribes, was a luxury enjoyed by the wealthy or reserved for feasts. It usually came from goats and sheep. The mainstay of the diet was grains and legumes (broad beans and lentils). Simple flatbreads were prepared from wheat or barley and baked on hot stones over fire by the nomadic shepherds, while farmers favored leavened breads. Grains were also toasted, cracked and used for stews and porridges, similarly to modern-day bulgur. Milk, usually goat and sheep, was used to make butter, cheese and sour-milk products. Vegetables such as turnips, leeks and cucumbers were eaten raw or cooked, although a vegetable garden required irrigation and was considered a luxury. Wild herbs (parsley, coriander, mustard, garlic and hyssop) were used to enrich and spice up food. ▷

The main source of sweetness was fruit: pomegranates, figs, dates, grapes, pears, quince and apricots. Dates, figs and grapes were dried and used to make molasses. Wild bee honey is mentioned several times in the Bible, but many scholars believe that "honey" (*dvash*) in the "Land of Milk and Honey" refers to date molasses, currently called *silan*.

Olive oil was of paramount importance — used for cooking and dressing food, for lighting, in cosmetics and in religious rituals. Last but not least — wine. Consumed daily, mixed with water and often spiced, the elixir of love and deceit, wine became an integral part of Jewish life and worship. Here again one can see the schism between shepherds and farmers: the shepherds shunned wine, considered a typical part of the diet of the rival peasant tribes.

The Diaspora

What became known as Jewish cuisine, or rather Jewish cuisines, bears little resemblance to the Biblical legacy. They evolved during two thousand years in the Diaspora that began when the Jews were exiled from the Land of Israel in the first centuries AD and scattered far and wide. Jewish communities maintained autonomous lifestyles but were deeply influenced by the foods and cooking of the cultures in which they lived. Jewish Moroccan cuisine closely resembles that of Muslim Moroccans, and Jewish Polish cooking is not that different from that of their non-Jewish neighbors.

The differences arose from the laws of kashrut that shun certain foodstuffs (seafood, pork) and forbid the mixing of dairy and meat. The law that prohibits work on the Sabbath (Shabbat) led to the creation of casseroles that cook on residual heat lit before the Sabbath. Gefilte fish was devised so fish could be eaten without the need to remove bones — considered work and therefore prohibited on Shabbat. But Shabbat was not just about prohibitions, it was the day on which even the poorest indulged in a good meal, even if it meant doing without for the rest of the week.

Even more colorful and varied is Jewish holiday cooking. A festive meal is often the culmination of religious celebrations, be it the ritual Passover Seder, a New Year's eve (Rosh Hashanah) dinner, or a meal taken in a makeshift hut during the week-long Feast of the Tabernacles (Sukkot). Deep-fried sweetmeats commemorate the miracle of oil at Hanukkah, honey-laden, caramelized meat and vegetable dishes celebrate Rosh Hashanah, lamb casseroles announce Passover…the variety is endless, with every community giving its own interpretation of the festive menu.

One cannot discuss Jewish food without addressing the different worlds of Sephardic and Ashkenazi Jews. What ▷

Jerusalem: From Middle Eastern sweets, to authentic market eateries — a wealth of culinary traditions of the ancient capital

Sephardic communities that arrived in Jerusalem as early as the 17th Century preserved dishes originating in Spain and enhanced them with influences from the Ottoman kitchen, creating what is known today as Jerusalem Cuisine.

Galilee: sunset on the Sea of Galilee; opposite: goats at a dairy farm

For inspiration the early settlers looked to their Arab neighbors, whose appearance and lifestyle they felt represented the continuation of the Biblical Hebrews. Incidentally, they were not mistaken, as current research indicates.

◁ is known as "Jewish food" is in fact Russian-Polish Jewish cooking, introduced to the West by the massive migration of Jews to Western Europe and The United States at the end of the 19th and the beginning of the 20th Centuries. Borscht, gefilte fish, chopped liver and chicken soup are among the best known Askenazi fare, but there is much more, including the rich dishes of Hungarian Jews and the piquant Jewish Romanian cuisine influenced by the neighboring Balkans. Sephardic Jewish cuisines are even more diverse, though much less known outside their respective communities. Claudia Roden in her monumental work, "The Book of Jewish Food", refers to them as "secret cuisines" of the world. According to Roden, these were hedonistic culinary cultures "less concerned with inner, spiritual life than the Ashkenazi, more sensitive to beauty and pleasure". *Sepharad* means Spain in Hebrew, and one of the most prominent Sephardic cuisines is that of Jews exiled from Spain in the 15th Century and dispersed in the Balkans and the Ottoman Empire. Sephardic communities that arrived in Jerusalem as early as the 17th Century preserved and perfected dishes originating in Spain and enhanced them with influences from the Ottoman kitchen, creating what is known today as Jerusalem Cuisine. Stuffed vegetables, dainty sweetmeats and bourekas are among its hallmarks.

And yet this is just the tip of the iceberg. There are the spicy cuisines of North African Jews (Moroccan, Lybian, Tunisian and Algerian), unique ancient cuisines of Iraqi, Kurdish and Persian Jews, and a host of wonderful dishes that evolved in Syria, Lebanon, Yemen and India. The common denominator of all these traditions is the centrality of food to the celebration of any family event. Holidays, weddings, the birth of a baby, a bar mitzvah — all are marked by one or more elaborate meals whose preparation can occupy the family, mainly the women, for weeks on end.

The Return to the Land of Israel

Jewish immigration to Palestine commenced with the advent of the Zionist Movement at the end of the 19th Century. The first waves of immigrants came from Russia and later from Poland and other East European countries, joined in the 1930s by German Jews fleeing the Nazi Regime.

The early settlers were idealistic youngsters driven by the vision of building a homeland for their long-suffering people.

Their dream was to create a new Israeli who will speak Hebrew and work the land, who will be tough and strong and able to defend himself. This meant severing ties with the recent past — ones representing suffering and humiliation: the language, music, customs and food of the Diaspora. For inspiration the early settlers looked to their Arab neighbors, whose appearance and lifestyle they felt represented the continuation of the Biblical Hebrews. Incidentally, they were not mistaken as current research indicates that Arab peasants and shepherds have indeed preserved many culinary traditions that go back to the age of Biblical Israel.

The striving for the new identity was especially evident in the kibbutz, collective settlements with no private ownership. Kibbutzniks wore khaki shorts and sandals, suitable to the Mediterranean climate. They spoke Hebrew and ate what they grew and produced by the sweat of their brow. The Israeli breakfast, perhaps the most famous local culinary institution, evolved in their communal dining rooms.

The cities were a different story. The German and central Europe immigrants of the 1930s settled in the cities and on *moshavim*, farm cooperatives with private ownership of land and homes. They brought European habits like Viennese coffee, strudel and Wiener schnitzel, and their lifestyle and diet looked more to Europe than the Levant. The coffeehouse took root in Tel Aviv and Jerusalem, where a bohemian culture grew alongside the literary elite, lending high status to this new ethos. ▷

kibbutzniks still remember WIZO instructors trying to teach them how to liven up the bland cooking that was the norm.

The Melting Pot

Jews who came from Arab countries and North Africa in the late '40s and early '50s obviously needed no education in Middle Eastern ingredients: their problems were different. Over one million immigrants, mainly from Arab countries but also European Holocaust survivors, flooded the new State of Israel, whose population at the time was no more than 800,000 and was still recovering from the ravages of the 1948 War of Independence. Sephardic Jews were often looked down on by the settlers of European origin, both veteran and newcomers. They spoke different languages, had darker skin, cooked and spiced their food differently, and followed strange customs. They arrived at a time of economic hardship, of rationing (*tsena*), when only basic foods were available. Cherished ethnic dishes had to be modified: eggplant made to taste like chopped liver for the East Europeans; kubbe made from frozen fish instead of ground meat for the Iraqis; kicheri, a stew of rice and lentils now eaten with ptitim, toasted pasta flakes invented at the time of *tsena* as a substitute for rice. Ethnic groups clung tenaciously to their culinary heritage, partly as a way of preserving their identity, but a certain amount of interaction began to take place. Recipes and cooking advice were swapped. The first steps towards a multi-ethnic food culture were underway.

If the ethos of the kibbutz was to create a simple local tradition, a new ethos was born in the late 1960s and 1970s when Israel opened up to the rest of the world: to resemble as much as possible that bigger melting pot, America. It is not surprising that Ruth Sirkis's 1974 cookbook "From the Kitchen with Love" made such an impact on Israeli food culture. Sirkis was living in Boston around the time Julia Child was teaching Americans about French cooking. She brought to Israel the missing element — international French-style cooking with an emphasis on dining out. This was soon followed by Chinese, Italian and French restaurants that sprang up from Kiryat Shmona in the North to Eilat in the South.

The more local style of dining out was found in *misadot mizrachiyot*, literally eastern restaurants. These popularly priced establishments served a basic selection of meze salads followed by grilled meat with a side order of French fries and a chocolate mousse for desert. Though many were run by Arabs, there was almost no hint of authentic Palestinian cooking. With the exception of hummus and falafel, which by that time had acquired the status of "national food", Israelis knew very little about what their Arab neighbors eat. ▷

◁ Ideology aside, urban housewives and *kibbutz* cooks had quite a few problems in common. Produce was scarce and of poor quality, culinary know-how nonexistent. Even those who didn't reject Diaspora food in principle had little use for East European recipes, ill-suited to the hot Mediterranean climate. The first Zionist cookbook, published in the 1930s and printed in Hebrew, English and German, sheds light on the culinary dilemmas of the time. The title says it all: "How to Cook in Palestine". The author, Dr. Erna Meyer, had a heartfelt message for her readers: "We housewives must make an attempt to free our kitchens from European customs which are not appropriate to Palestine. We should wholeheartedly stand in favour of healthy Palestinian cooking. We should foster these ideas not merely because we are compelled to do so, but because we realize that it will help us more than anything else in becoming acclimatized to our old-new homeland…." The style may be archaic but the culinary advice that followed is very up-to date. Meyer recommends growing Mediterranean herbs on a windowsill and getting acquainted with Middle Eastern spices that can do wonders for the blandest of ingredients; and she cajoles cooks from Berlin and Warsaw to include "exotic" vegetables like courgettes, eggplants, olives, okra and leeks in their menus. The book was published by the Palestine Federation of WIZO (Women's International Zionist Organization), which was very active in culinary education of the population; veteran

Open-air markets brim with fresh produce, spices and rare condiments

Meyer recommends getting acquainted with spices that can do wonders for the blandest of ingredients, and she cajoles cooks from Berlin and Warsaw to include "exotic" vegetables like courgettes, eggplants, okra and leeks in their menus.

began to travel abroad, developing an appetite not only for the trappings of the good life but also for new foods and wines. The ethos of a people struggling under austere conditions gradually gave way before a desire for creature comforts. The ideal of a melting pot that would ultimately yield the consummate Israeli gave way to the ethos of a heterogeneous society in which each ethnic group was entitled to cultivate its heritage.

In the late 1980s Tsachi Buchshester opened "Hatarvad Havarod" (The Pink Ladle), followed shortly by Itamar Davidoff who launched "Pitango", both in Tel Aviv. The innovative dishes created in these tiny, experimental restaurants were the first attempts to fuse international cuisine with Middle Eastern influences. Buchshester's halva parfait is a good example: the technique is French, the main ingredient is Middle Eastern, the result — the most fashionable, widely imitated dessert of the '80s. Around the same time Eyal Shani opened "Oceanus" in Jerusalem aimed at haute cuisine showcasing local ingredients; eggplants and tomatoes, tahini

Haim Cohen: "Why should restaurant chefs make one kind of food for their diners, while they themselves prefer to eat something completely different? It doesn't make sense. My goal is to fuse the friendly food that we love so much with fine dining".

◁ Ethnic Jewish cooking was also poorly represented. Ashkenazi restaurants did exist here and there, but the exquisite Sephardic cuisines were enjoyed mainly at home. There were exceptions: a few restaurants in the Yemenite Quarter of Tel Aviv; several Balkan restaurants in Jaffa where many Bulgarian Jews had settled in the early '50s; and quite a few fine eating places in Jerusalem that served the flagship dishes of Sephardic Jerusalem cuisine: sofrito, kubbe, stuffed vegetables and the like.

With dining out becoming more popular, local chefs felt the need to create something of their own. In the 1970s a number of them endeavored to develop an Israeli haute cuisine, applying French techniques to Israeli food icons like oranges, avocados and bananas. The results were dishes with patriotic names, like "Banana Tel Kazir" or "Fish in Mishmar Hayarden Sauce" (two settlements that suffered heavy bombing prior to the Six Day War). These creations had little impact on the general public and remained confined to hotel cooking.

In the mid 1980s several factors came together to completely revolutionize the local food scene. The peace treaty signed with Egypt in 1979 brought a feeling of hope and optimism, the economy was getting better, and the average citizen

and wild herbs were the stars of his menu and were treated with the respect reserved for fancier foodstuffs.

In 1989 chef Haim Cohen and Irit Shenkar launched "Keren" in Jaffa with the dream of creating a high-class restaurant on a par with the best New York and London had to offer. In the early days the menu was predominantly French, but as Cohen gained confidence, he became more daring. Lamb kebab with tahini in an ultra-premium restaurant? Shakshuka (a simple egg dish of Lybian origin) with foie gras? The public, skeptical at first, was quickly seduced. It simply felt right. "Food, like culture, doesn't travel well," said Cohen in an interview for a trade magazine. "We go to France, feast on French food and bring home tons of French cheeses, but they get stuck in the fridge. When we come home we crave labane and a vegetable salad. Why should restaurant chefs make one kind of food for their diners, while they themselves prefer to eat something completely different? It doesn't make sense. My goal is to fuse the friendly food that we love so much with fine dining".

Erez Komarovsky, probably the most influential figure on the current Israeli food scene, also studied abroad and came back a passionate advocate of local food: "We all went ▷

14

Manta Ray, Tel Aviv: Mediterranean cuisine
where it belongs — by the sea

Tel Aviv: Rothschild Boulevard, favorite meeting place for the young, is dotted with coffee shops. Opposite: Raphael (top) and Food Art are among the best restaurants in the city.

◁ abroad, but we all decided to come back. I returned because I like using fresh lemon juice and olive oil more than butter and soy sauce. I prefer hyssop and thyme to European herbs, I enjoy red mullets more than langoustines, and connect better to shawarma than to steak tartare."

Paradoxically, as Israeli society becomes more cosmopolitan and sophisticated in its tastes, local ethnic food traditions become more pronounced. Family heritage is often the primary source of inspiration for local chefs. Rafi Cohen, owner-chef of "Raphael" in Tel Aviv, incorporates dishes from the kitchen of his Moroccan grandmother. Ezra Kedem of "Arcadia" in Jerusalem fuses his family's Iraqi cookery with techniques he learned in New York; he works exclusively with local ingredients and shops mainly in the nearby Mahane-Yehuda Market. Regardless of their ethnic origin, leading Israeli chefs all offer some kind of personal take on Mediterranean and Middle Eastern cuisines. Many Arab-owned restaurants followed suit and now include authentic Palestinian dishes on their menus, showing the Jewish population that their cuisine is not all about hummus and shish-kebab.

Obviously the local food renaissance is not confined to restaurants. All good cooking starts with ingredients, and here the change is equally dramatic. In 1983 Golan Heights Winery went into production, heralding a new age for Israeli wines. A few years earlier the boutique cheese producers came on stream. Olive oil became a sought-after product following many years of neglect. Highly developed marine aquaculture ensures the steady supply of fresh saltwater fish, and the choice and quality of fresh fruit, vegetables and herbs is simply overwhelming.

Home cooking greatly benefits from this abundance. A new generation of amateur cooks no longer confine themselves to the dishes they learned at home, and cross-overs between different ethnic groups are the norm. On the Friday night dinner table in the average Israeli home, chicken soup coexists happily with spicy Moroccan fish, and a chicken schnitzel is served on a bed of couscous.

Is there such a thing as Israeli cuisine? This question, frequently discussed in the media, is clearly premature. A society of immigrants from more than 70 countries, Israel is constantly changing, and so is its cuisine. The food culture that has evolved is one of dynamic cross-fertilization between numerous influences: Arab and Jewish, Eastern Europe and North Africa, religious and secular, new immigrants and old-timers, locals and foreigners. They all work together to create a synergy that is Israeli food today. Fusion is the essence and the journey goes on. And what a delicious voyage!

Paradoxically, as Israeli society becomes more cosmopolitan and sophisticated in its tastes, local ethnic food traditions become more pronounced. Family heritage is often the primary source of inspiration for local chefs.

salads etc.

The Israeli Salad

Take a few cucumbers, some firm ripe tomatoes, an onion and a couple of sweet red peppers. The proper Israeli way is to dice everything fine and neat (*dak-dak*, very fine, or *katan-katan*, very small), but coarsely cut chunks will do just fine. Add some fresh herbs like chopped parsley, coriander, chives, spring onions, or even chopped mint if you are feeling adventurous. Squeeze lemon juice, sprinkle virgin olive oil, season with salt and ground black pepper, toss everything together and serve.

There you have it, the Israeli Salad: healthy, wholesome, simple and delicious. A fine dish to be sure, but what is so characteristically Israeli about it? Similar salads are served all over the Eastern Mediterranean, from Greece to Lebanon. In fact, most Israeli restaurants call this Arab Salad, which is probably more accurate.

The answer must be that most of us simply cannot do without it. Israelis insist on a salad with almost every meal. At breakfast they will go to great lengths to prepare their salad just right to have with scrambled or fried eggs, green olives and cottage cheese. At lunch it is the natural side dish, whatever the main course. Even if you are having your lunch on the go, stuffed in a pita, the salad goes in there too, along with French fries, in what is known locally as *chipsalat*. Israelis will order a salad at a seaside restaurant with grilled fish, in a steak house with barbecued beef or chicken, and even as a snack at a fashionable café. A

somewhat neglected Israeli ritual consists of a light summer supper on the balcony, in the evening breeze. Invariably, the centerpiece is a huge bowl of freshly made, finely diced vegetable salad with an omelet, fresh white cheese (*gvina levana*), and soft white bread (preferably challah) to mop up the delicious juices left at the bottom of the bowl.

The secret to a great Israeli salad is no secret at all: choose ripe and flavorful vegetables, make sure they are room temperature (refrigeration dulls their flavor), use a very sharp knife to avoid crushing or mashing the vegetables, season heartily and serve promptly.

To perk up the flavor of your salad, sprinkle a dash of ground cinnamon (yes!) in addition to salt and pepper, and add some diced fresh lemon.

Our Favorite Israeli Salad

Make sure the vegetables are room temperature. If you keep your vegetables in the refrigerator, take them out half an hour before preparation.

Ingredients (serves 2-4)

1 juicy lemon, halved
4 firm ripe tomatoes, diced
4 unpeeled cucumbers, diced
1 red onion, finely diced
1 sweet red pepper, seeded and diced
1 clove garlic, crushed
1/2 fresh hot green pepper, seeded and chopped (optional)

Dash cinnamon
1 teaspoon sumac (optional)
Salt and freshly ground black pepper to taste
3 tablespoons extra virgin olive oil
2-3 tablespoons parsley and/or coriander and/or mint leaves, chopped

1. Squeeze the juice of half the lemon. Remove the pips from the remaining half and peel the skin (including the white pulp). Chop finely.
2. Place the chopped lemon and the lemon juice in a bowl, add the remaining ingredients and toss. Taste and adjust the seasoning. Serve immediately.

For a more delicate texture, use peeled tomatoes. With a sharp knife, nick the skin on the bottom of each tomato in the form of a cross, drop into boiling water for 30 seconds, remove and peel off the skins.

Variations Take advantage of choice seasonal vegetables to make your salad even more wholesome: coarsely grated carrots, finely sliced cabbage (red or white), and chopped young radishes, fennel bulbs, spring onions and chives.

Fatoush Salad

Anyone who likes the juices of a vegetable salad is bound to love this one, which is based on a combination of tomatoes, olive oil and lemon. Chunks of toasted pita bread absorb the delicious juices and add crunch.

Ingredients (serves 2-4)

3 firm ripe tomatoes, cut into small chunks
3 cucumbers, cut into small chunks
1 onion, chopped
1 large or 4 small radishes, grated (optional)
1/3 cup fresh coriander, chopped
1/3 cup fresh mint, chopped
1/3 cup fresh parsley, chopped

2 tablespoons lemon juice
2-3 cloves garlic, crushed
5 tablespoons olive oil
Salt and freshly ground black pepper to taste
2 pita breads (stale ones can be used)

1. Brush the pita breads lightly with olive oil and toast them in a hot oven or on a charcoal grill until golden brown. Cool and break into large chunks.
2. Mix the rest of the ingredients, add the pita chunks, toss everything together and adjust the seasoning. Serve immediately.

Tomato Fatoush (see photo on the opposite page) Follow the recipe for Fatoush, but use only tomatoes cut in wedges and 2 sliced red onions. Omit the rest of the vegetables.

Water Salad

Basically a vegetable salad, with dry mint adding a zing. The ice water turns this salad into a kind of cold soup.

Ingredients (serves 2-4)

2 tomatoes, diced
2 unpeeled cucumbers, diced
3 cloves garlic, chopped
5 tablespoons fresh parsley, chopped

1 teaspoon dry mint
5 tablespoons lemon juice
5 tablespoons olive oil
Salt and freshly ground black pepper

1. Mix all the ingredients in a bowl.
2. Cover with ice water to the level of the contents and refrigerate for one hour.
3. Serve with a spoon — this salad should be eaten with the water.

"Everything" Salad

Orna Agmon and Ella Shine, Orna & Ella, Tel Aviv

Tomatoes, cucumbers, lettuce and rocket, feta cheese, sourdough bread croutons and a wonderfully creamy dressing . . . waiters at Orna & Ella, tired of reciting the goodies in this salad, simply state that it has "everything". The name stuck and the "everything" salad evolved into one of the most popular dishes in this much-loved Tel Aviv establishment.

Ingredients (serves 4-6)

The Creamy Herb Dressing:
1 cup fresh mint
1/2 cup fresh basil
1 cup fresh parsley
1/4 cup chives
1 cup mayonnaise (preferably homemade)
100 ml (4 oz, 1/2 small container) sour cream
Salt and freshly ground black pepper
The Salad:
4-5 tomatoes, diced

3-4 cucumbers, peeled and diced
A large handful of garden rocket leaves, shredded
6 leaves romaine lettuce, shredded
2-3 tablespoons fresh parsley, coarsely chopped
2-3 tablespoons fresh mint, coarsely chopped
To Serve:
200 g (7 oz) feta cheese, cut into cubes
Croutons (see below)

1. **Prepare the dressing:** Purée the herbs and the sour cream in a food processor. Add the mayonnaise, season with salt and pepper and mix well. The dressing will keep in the refrigerator up to 2 days.
2. **Assemble the salad:** Mix the vegetables, lettuce, rocket and herbs and transfer to a shallow bowl. Spoon on a few tablespoons of the dressing, sprinkle feta cheese and croutons on top and serve at once.

Croutons At Orna & Ella croutons are made from the delicious breads baked on the premises, but any fine bread (preferably sourdough) will do. Cut the bread into 1cm (1/2 inch) cubes, put in a bowl and sprinkle with olive oil, salt and pepper. Toss with your hands and spread in a single layer on a baking tray lined with baking paper. Bake in a 170°C (325°F) oven for 35-40 minutes, until the croutons are crisp and golden. Store in an airtight jar.

Eggplant

A common Arab adage goes something like this: "If your future bride can't prepare eggplant fifty different ways — don't marry her!" Indeed, this sexy-looking member of the potato family may be savored hot or cold, grilled, barbecued, deep fried, sautéed, roasted, baked, stuffed, marinated, pickled, in pastry, casseroles, stews and even confitures and jams. Its flesh, grilled or roasted on an open flame, may be used in an infinite variety of salads and dips. It welcomes a vast range of seasonings and flavors, from sweet, sweet and sour and mild mayonnaise-like flavors, through aggressive vinegar, onion and garlic combinations, to extremely spicy, palate-scorching Middle Eastern style flavoring. It blends particularly well with lemon and garlic, as well as with yogurt, tahini, feta cheese, various herbs, raw and fried onions, tomatoes and many other vegetables. In fact, it is so versatile that one Israeli cookbook describes a complete meal (appetizers, starters, entrées, main courses, side dishes, salads, pickles, pastries and desserts) made entirely of, or with, eggplants.

It seems eggplants have always been around in Israel. When the first Zionist settlers came to these parts in the late 19th Century, they were quick to adopt a variety of Middle Eastern, especially Turkish, eggplant dishes. In the early 1950s, when the fledgling State of Israel was struggling with rationing, eggplants were in relative abundance (unlike poultry, beef, eggs and dairy products). Newspapers and radio gave advice on how to make the most out of the foods available. And just as a major food manufacturer invented

toasted pasta (affectionately known as "Ben-Gurion's Rice", see p. 127), someone came up with "fake chopped liver" — an eggplant salad devised to simulate the texture, color and taste of chopped chicken liver. This particular dish, along with a similar salad made with courgettes, is still popular.

Current Israeli cuisine no longer regards eggplant as a substitute for something else, or as something to be disguised or camouflaged. On the contrary — it is revered and loved in its most basic form. The current vogue is to serve it whole, flame-roasted, with such complementary toppings as yogurt or tahini.

Eggplants are inexpensive and readily available year-round. Proper selection is not difficult: choose the ones that are lighter in weight and have firm, unblemished, shiny skin and green, fresh-looking leaves and stalks. Heavier eggplants may contain bitter seeds.

Flame-Roasting Eggplants

Roasting eggplants on an open flame can be messy but is definitely worth the effort as the smoky aroma adds immensely to the taste.

First line your stovetop with aluminum foil. Place a whole eggplant (or more than one if you are confident) on a rack over the open flame and roast, turning occasionally, until the skin is scorched and blackened and the flesh feels soft when pierced with a wooden skewer or a fork. The eggplant can also be broiled in the oven, or grilled on a charcoal barbecue. Cool slightly (to avoid burning your hands) and peel, carefully removing every last bit of scorched skin, or cut in half lengthwise and scoop out the flesh with a wooden spoon. Ideally, roasted eggplant should be served shortly after roasting, and seasoned while still warm to ensure optimal absorption of every spicy nuance. But if you need to store it for later, drain the roasted flesh of excess liquid, cover with oil and refrigerate. Season before serving.

31

Eggplants come in many shapes. Beside the familiar elongated kind, there are fan-like Balladi eggplants with sweet meaty flesh and very few seeds. The tiny ones are used for stuffing and pickling.

8 Dips and Salads with Roasted Eggplant

Roasted Eggplant with Yogurt For best results, use strongly flavored yogurt like that from goat or sheep milk.
Add 2 cups to the flesh of two roasted eggplants. Season with crushed garlic, salt and freshly ground black pepper. Chopped mint and coriander leaves may be added as well.

Roasted Eggplant with Tahini This classic combination always works. Use best quality tahini.
Add 1/2 cup raw tahini seasoned with 3-4 tablespoons lemon juice, 2 cloves crushed garlic, 2-3 tablespoons chopped parsley, a pinch of salt and freshly ground black pepper to the flesh of two roasted eggplants. If the mixture is too thick, add water gradually and stir to desired texture. Sprinkle with toasted sesame seeds or pine nuts before serving.

Roasted Eggplant with Yogurt and Tahini Adding both these last two ingredients produces a delightful dip.
Add 1 cup yogurt and 1/4 cup raw tahini to the flesh of two roasted eggplants. Season with two tablespoons chopped mint leaves, 2 tablespoons lemon juice, 2 cloves crushed garlic, salt and freshly ground black pepper. If the mixture is too thick, add water gradually and stir to desired texture.

Roasted Eggplant with Pecans and Blue Cheese This union of particularly strong flavors produces a delicious sandwich spread. Add about 1/2 cup crumbled blue (Roquefort style) cheese and 1/2 cup toasted chopped pecans to the flesh of two roasted eggplants.

Roasted Eggplant with Feta Add a crumbled chunk (about 200 grams, 7 oz) of cheese to the flesh of two roasted eggplants, along with 1/4 cup olive oil, some sumac or dried oregano leaves and 3 chopped spring onions.

Romanian-style Roasted Eggplant Salad Don't be alarmed by the amount of oil. The eggplants love it, and so do the Romanians.
Add 1/2 cup oil (the Romanians insist on strongly flavored sunflower oil, preferably unrefined), at least 3 cloves crushed garlic, salt and freshly ground black pepper to the flesh of two roasted eggplants. You may also add two grated onions and/or two peeled, grated tomatoes. To keep the texture pleasantly palatable rather than muddy, mix the oil with the other ingredients by stirring gently with a wooden spoon.

Roasted Eggplant with Red Peppers Bulgarian Jews call this salad Kiopolo
Add 2-3 flame-roasted sweet red peppers (peeled and chopped, see explanation on p. 54), 1/4 cup oil, 2 cloves crushed garlic and salt to the flesh of two roasted eggplants.

Roasted Eggplant with Pesto A dip with an Italian flair.
Add about 1/2 cup of pesto to the flesh of two roasted eggplants. If you make the pesto at home, try different mixtures of herbs, nuts and cheese. Similar dips can be made with tapenade (olive spread) or sun-dried tomato spread.

Eggplant Dip
Serving Suggestions

Eggplant Dip in Eggplant Skin
Cut a roasted eggplant in half and scoop out the flesh. Keep the skin intact. Prepare the eggplant dip of your choice, ladle it back into the empty skin and serve.

Phyllo Pastry Baskets with Eggplant Salad/Dip Brush several phyllo pastry sheets with olive oil and arrange in small, fairly deep baking dishes to form several cups. Bake in a hot oven until golden. Allow to cool, remove the pastry cups from the baking dishes, fill with your favorite eggplant dip.

Eggplant Rolls Thinly slice an eggplant lengthwise. Deep fry until golden. Drain on paper towel, allow to cool, fill with your favorite eggplant dip, roll and serve.

Bruschetta with Eggplant Dip Brush a few slices of bread (baguette or ciabatta) with olive oil. Toast in the oven or grill until brown and rub with a clove of garlic. Pile your favorite eggplant dip on top.

Roasted Eggplant and Goat Cheese Mousse

This tasty fluffy whip may be spread on a slice of freshly baked bread or served as the starter of an elegant meal.

Ingredients (serves 6-8)
3 eggplants
200 g (7 oz) soft goat cheese
1 cup whipping cream

2-3 drops Tabasco sauce
Salt and freshly ground black pepper

1. Roast the eggplants (see explanation on p. 31), cool slightly, peel and chop.
2. Whisk the cheese with 1/4 cup of the cream to a smooth paste. Transfer to a bowl and combine with the chopped eggplants.
3. Pour the remaining cream into a mixing bowl and whip into a soft whipped cream. Fold the whipped cream into the cheese and eggplant paste and season with Tabasco sauce, salt and pepper.
4. Serve promptly or keep refrigerated in a covered bowl for up to two days.

Roasted Eggplant and Goat Cheese Soup

Yaron Kestenbaum, Food Art Catering, Tel Aviv

Yet another delicious combination of eggplants and goat cheese.

Ingredients (serves 10)
1/3 cup olive oil
3 carrots, diced
2 onions, diced
1 leek (white part only), diced
3 cloves garlic, chopped
2 bay leaves
1/2 cup dry white wine
6 eggplants

2 cups milk
2 cups whipping cream
2-3 thyme sprigs
Salt and freshly ground black pepper
To serve:
170 g (6 oz) soft goat cheese
Seeds from 2 tomatoes
Small thyme sprigs

1. Roast the eggplants (see explanation on p. 31), cool slightly, peel and chop.
2. Heat the oil in a deep pan, add vegetables, garlic and bay leaves and sweat for 5 minutes. Add the wine, season with salt and pepper and cook over low heat until the liquid is reduced to a thick syrup.
3. Add the chopped eggplants, milk, cream and thyme sprigs, bring to a boil, reduce heat to a minimum and simmer for about an hour. Taste and adjust seasoning.
4. Purée the soup in a blender and pass through a fine sieve.
5. Ladle into serving bowls, crumble the goat cheese on top, add the tomato seeds and garnish with thyme sprigs.

Eggplant Carpaccio

Yaron Kestenbaum, Food Art Catering, Tel Aviv

A roasted eggplant served whole accompanied by various garnishes has evolved into one of the hallmarks of modern Israeli cuisine. This version, more a serving suggestion than a recipe, combines some of the local favorites in one delicious attractive dish — yogurt, tahini, olive oil, tomatoes, silan (date honey) and fresh hyssop leaves.

Ingredients (serves 4)

4 medium eggplants
4 tablespoons top quality raw tahini
4 tablespoons goat milk yogurt
4 tomatoes, halved
4 teaspoons silan or 3 teaspoons honey
4 tablespoons freshly squeezed lemon juice

8 tablespoons extra virgin olive oil
1 small bunch of fresh hyssop or oregano leaves
1 teaspoon crushed garlic
1 teaspoon chopped hot green pepper
Coarse sea salt and freshly ground black pepper

1. Roast the eggplants (see instructions on p. 31), cool slightly and cut open.
2. Place the eggplants in the center of 4 plates and flatten slightly with a fork.
3. Pour small puddles of tahini, yogurt, silan (or honey), olive oil and lemon juice over the eggplant. Spoon out the contents of one tomato over each eggplant. Season with salt, pepper, garlic and hot pepper. Garnish with hyssop or oregano leaves and serve immediately.

Tahini

The origin of the word tahini (or tahina) is Arabic *tahn*, literally meaning ground, similar to the Hebrew *tachun*. It is made from ground sesame seeds and has innumerable uses in Middle Eastern cuisine. It is the basic ingredient in various hummus dishes, serves as a cooking sauce for meat and fish, and is mixed with vegetables to make a variety of meze salads. Combined with sweeteners, usually honey or silan (date honey), it is the basis for many sweets. Halva, one of the best known Middle Eastern confectionary products, is also made from tahini. In the new Israeli cuisine, tahini is a star ingredient, frequently used raw together with olive oil and fresh herbs.

The key to a successful tahini dish is choosing top quality raw material. The best locally made tahini comes from Arab towns, notably Nablus and Nazereth. Quality raw tahini is delicious on its own without any additions. Taste it straight from the jar. It should be nutty and slightly sweet, without a trace of bitterness.

Tahini and halva factory in Kefar Arra,
an Arab village in the Ara Valley

Tahini Dip

The most basic way to enjoy tahini's nutty flavor is to prepare a dip. It takes only a few minutes and requires no special equipment. Once you have made it at home using the best raw tahini, you will never again touch the ready-made variety. Serve the dip with warm pita bread, alongside hummus dishes, meze salads, falafel, and the like.

Ingredients (server 4-6)
1 cup top quality raw tahini
1-2 tablespoons freshly squeezed lemon juice

2-3 cloves garlic, crushed (optional)
Salt to taste

Whisk all the ingredients in a large bowl and gradually add ice-cold water. Don't be alarmed when the first bit of water makes the paste thick and lumpy. Keep whisking and adding liquid and the mixture will get thinner and silky smooth. The amount of water depends on the desired consistency: 1/2 cup for a thick tahini dip, 1 cup or even a bit more for a thin sauce suitable for pouring over vegetables or falafel.

Green Tahini Dip Add 1/2 cup parsley, 1/4 cup coriander and 1/4 cup mint, all chopped, to the basic tahini dip recipe.
Nutty Tahini Dip Add 1/2 cup coarsely ground pistachio nuts or walnuts to the basic tahini dip recipe.
For More Substantial Quantities Use a blender. Bear in mind that blending heats the tahini, so use ice cubes instead of water. This will keep the tahini white and ensure a pleasant, stable texture.

Baked Lamb Patties in Tahini Sauce

The inspiration for this recipe is siniya, one of the flagship dishes of Palestinian cuisine — ground lamb baked in tahini. For best results, get yourself a siniya baking pan, a round ovenproof pan in which the dish is baked and served. Or prepare it in a baking dish or a shallow ovenproof saucepan.

Ingredients for 20 large patties (serves 6-7)

1 kg (2 lb 4 oz) ground lamb (with some fat)
2 onions, chopped
3 cloves garlic, crushed
1 heaping tablespoon baharat spice mix (p. 299)
2 tablespoons olive oil
1/2 cup fresh parsley or coriander, chopped

The Tahini sauce:
1/2 cup raw tahini
2 tablespoons freshly squeezed lemon juice
Salt and freshly ground black pepper
1/2 teaspoon ground cumin
2-3 tablespoons pine nuts
To Serve:
Fresh chopped mint

1. **Prepare the patties:** Mix the meat with the onions, garlic, parsley or coriander, baharat and olive oil. Knead thoroughly and refrigerate for 30 minutes.
2. Heat the oven to 220°C (425°F).
3. Knead again and form large flat patties. Arrange in a siniya pan or ovenproof pan and bake for 10 minutes.
4. **While the patties are baking, prepare the sauce:** Whisk the raw tahini with one cup of water — the sauce should be smooth and quite thin. Add the lemon juice and season to taste.
5. Pour the sauce over the partly baked patties. Sprinkle the pine nuts and bake for 10-15 minutes until the tahini sauce forms a crust over the patties. Garnish with chopped mint and serve immediately.

Sea Bass Fillet in Raw Tahini Sauce

Aviv Moshe, Messa, Tel Aviv

Use the best quality tahini for this simple tasty dish.

Ingredients (serves 4)

8 fillets of sea bass or other portion-sized white flesh saltwater fish
3/4 cup extra virgin olive oil
8 tablespoons fresh oregano leaves
4-5 tablespoons freshly squeezed lemon juice

1 cup raw tahini
4 teaspoons persimmon, cut into small dice
8 filleted orange segments (see instructions on p. 61)
Coarse sea salt

1. Heat 1 tablespoon olive oil in a heavy skillet and fry the fish fillets for 2 minutes on each side. Keep warm.
2. Heat the remaining olive oil in a saucepan for 2 minutes, add oregano and remove from the stove.
3. Arrange 2 fillets on each serving plate, pour over the raw tahini and hot olive oil with herbs. Sprinkle some lemon juice.
4. Garnish with persimmons and orange fillets, sprinkle sea salt and serve immediately.

Hummus

Take any Israeli, especially one of the male gender, and he may rave about his mother's cooking or brag about a terrific restaurant he has been to recently. But, when pressed, the overwhelming majority of Israelis will admit that hummus is their favorite food.

Israelis hold hummus in such high regard that it is rarely made at home. Instead, it is savored — or rather worshipped — at a favorite *hummusia*. This humble establishment offers only this sacred concoction, with a limited selection of extras: tahini, hard-boiled eggs, a variety of pickles. A spicy lemon and garlic sauce and pita bread are mandatory.

Volumes have been written on the comparative virtues of the styles and traditions of hummus. There are those who prefer the light, smooth and fluffy Jerusalem-style hummus, while others swear by the spicier chunkier Galilee version. One particularly vocal group proclaims the virtues of the heavier, more substantial hummus of Jaffa, while others will settle for nothing but the creamy hummus made in Akko (Old Acre).

There are known-only-to-locals (but nevertheless nationally famous) hummus joints at gas stations, on side streets, in market alleys and in out-of-the-way villages. Surprisingly, spiffy upscale hummus restaurants have sprung up recently in the most prestigious neighborhoods and shopping centers and there is even one that serves organic hummus.

Made of boiled chickpeas, tahini, garlic, lemon and spices, hummus is regarded as a filling and nutritious "morning food". Real hummus is made fresh daily and does not keep. Indeed, most hummus places are closed by noon.

Every supermarket offers scores of commercial varieties of hummus, sporting various flavors, toppings and catchy names. Some of them are marginally palatable, but as every hummus devotée knows, they are a far cry from the real thing: freshly made hummus without preservatives, fillers or stabilizers, served promptly without refrigeration.

At this point you may ask, "Why not make hummus in the comfort of your own home?" Admittedly, the real thing calls for a mortar and pestle (hence the percussive sound heard at authentic hummus joints), but a household food processor will do quite nicely. The rest is fairly simple.

Guidelines for Hummus Novices

Tahini The most important factor in the making of a delicious hummus is the tahini. It should be top quality, made of 100% sesame seeds. To identify a really good tahini, taste it straight from the jar. It should have a smooth, slightly sweet, nutty taste, with no bitterness.

Chickpeas Dry chickpeas are the correct base for the dip, but canned or frozen chickpeas may be used and will save preparation time. Smaller chickpeas (locally called *das*) are better than larger ones.

Baking Soda (sodium bicarbonate) is usually added to the chickpeas during soaking and boiling to speed up the process and guarantee complete softening.

Storing Homemade hummus spoils quickly, especially during the summer. It will keep for up to two days in the refrigerator, but the whole point of making hummus at home is to enjoy it fresh and warm. So prepare small batches and serve within the hour.

Serving The basic fresh hummus dip is a delicious snack on its own, but to enjoy it fully, serve it with all the traditional trimmings and make sure your pita bread is oven fresh.

Hummus Hall of Fame: Sayid in Old Acre (top) and Abu Hassan (a.k.a. Ali Karawan) in Jaffa

Basic Hummus Dip

Ingredients (serves 8-10)

1/2 kg (1 lb 2 oz) small dry chickpeas
1 tablespoon + 1/2 teaspoon baking soda
1 cup raw top quality tahini

1 tablespoon freshly squeezed lemon juice
2 cloves garlic, crushed
Salt to taste

1. Soak the chickpeas overnight in a large bowl of cold water with one tablespoon of baking soda.
2. Drain and rinse the chickpeas and put them in a large pan. Add water until it reaches 2-3 cm (1 inch) above the chickpeas. Add the remaining 1/2 teaspoon of baking soda and bring to a boil. Cook covered over low heat for 2-3 hours, until the chickpeas are very soft. Cool slightly, drain and save some of the cooking liquid.
3. Put the chickpeas in a food processor, add 2/3 cup of the tahini and process until almost smooth. If the paste is too thick, add a few tablespoons of the cooking liquid. Season with lemon, garlic and salt; taste and adjust the seasoning. For a richer creamier version, add the remaining tahini and process until the hummus is completely smooth and fluffy.

Galilee Style Hummus Set aside 1 cup of cooked chickpeas. Purée the rest with 1/2 cup of raw tahini and the seasonings. Add the whole chickpeas and mix, slightly mashing the chickpeas. The texture should remain somewhat chunky.

Complete Hummus

This dip with all the trimmings is the royal flush of the hummus aficionado.

Ingredients (serves 6-8)

Basic hummus dip (recipe above)
The Sauce:
1 cup freshly squeezed lemon juice
2 teaspoons ground cumin
1 teaspoon salt
1 teaspoon hot red pepper, chopped
1 tablespoon garlic, crushed

4-5 Shipka peppers (small hot green, pickled peppers), seeded and chopped
To Serve:
Raw tahini
Olive oil
Chopped fresh parsley
Chopped onion

1. Mix the ingredients for the sauce and set aside for one hour.
2. Spoon 2-3 heaping tablespoons of hummus dip into each serving plate and spread around the rim, leaving a crater in the center. Fill the crater with one tablespoon of raw tahini. Pour on 2-3 tablespoons of the sauce, sprinkle some olive oil and top with chopped parsley and onion.

Complete Hummus with Whole Chickpeas Add 2-3 tablespoons of warm cooked chickpeas to each plate of hummus dip. Pour the sauce and the olive oil on top and serve with chopped parsley and onion.

Messabaha

Called *mashaushe* in the Galilee, this dish is served at most hummus joints and is easy to prepare at home. It is a mixture of warm cooked chickpeas with tahini and a piquant sauce.

Ingredients (serves 6)

6 cups cooked chickpeas (as prepared in the Basic Hummus Dip p. 47), warm
1 cup raw tahini
The Sauce:
6 tablespoons olive oil

3-4 tablespoons lemon juice
2 teaspoons ground cumin
1 teaspoon salt
1 hot red pepper, chopped
1 tablespoon garlic, crushed

1. Mix sauce ingredients and set aside.
2. Using a wooden spoon, mix warm chickpeas with tahini, mashing lightly.
3. Divide the mixture between 6 plates, pour the sauce over and serve immediately.

Hummus with Ful (Broad Beans)

One of the best-loved hummus combinations, a favorite morning booster of truckers, cabbies and anyone with thirty minutes to spare. Heap the boiled broad beans on a plate of hummus dip and serve with a hard-boiled egg.

Ingredients (serves 8)

200 g (7 oz) dry broad (fava) beans, soaked overnight in water and drained
1 teaspoon ground cumin
3 tablespoons olive oil
3 tablespoons freshly squeezed lemon juice

3 cloves garlic, crushed
Salt to taste
To Serve:
Basic Hummus Dip (p. 47)
Hard-boiled eggs

1. Put the broad beans in a large pan and add water to about 5 cm (2 inches) above the beans. Bring to a boil, cover and cook over low heat for a minimum of 3 hours, until the beans become very soft and turn almost into a mash. Mix occasionally and add water if necessary.
2. Season the hot mash with ground cumin, olive oil, lemon juice, garlic and salt. Heap on top of the hummus dip and serve with hard-boiled eggs.

Meze

"Let's start you off with some salads", the waiter will announce (rather than suggest). In fact, sometimes there is no warning at all. The table just fills up in a matter of minutes with a battery of tiny plates brimming with fresh and cooked vegetable salads, pickles, creamy hummus and tahini dips, snow-white labane cheese with a glistening puddle of olive oil, cracked green olives, taramasalata, marinated fish . . . the list goes on and on according to the season, the style of the restaurant and the generosity of the owners. A basket of warm pita bread will invariably be placed on the table, and if you're not careful you might end up waiving the rest of the meal.

Meze is the proper name for this plethora of flavors and colors, though trendy restaurants might call it antipasti, tappas or small plates, depending on the latest fashion in the dining world. Regardless of the name, the concept is Middle Eastern to the core: a hospitable lavish welcome that titillates the senses and sets the tone for more exciting dishes to come.

Laying a truly magnificent meze table is not so difficult, since nearly all the dishes are made ahead and you can always complement the selection with a few purchases: olives, a slab of feta cheese, pickled cucumbers and stuffed vine leaves. Don't forget the hummus and tahini dips, without which no meze table is complete. Make sure you have plenty of oven-fresh pita bread, as the proper way to enjoy the meze is to mop up (or "wipe" as we say in Israel) hummus, tahini and the like with a piece of pita.

Turkish Salad

This red piquant booster to your pita is prepared with fresh vegetables that "cook" in the refrigerator.

Ingredients (serves 4-6)

1 large onion, chopped	1 tablespoon tomato paste
2 tomatoes, diced finely	11/2 tablespoons ketchup
2/3 cup fresh parsley, chopped	Salt and freshly ground black pepper
1 sweet red pepper, diced	1 tablespoon olive oil

1. Mix the onion, tomatoes and chopped parsley and add the red pepper, tomato paste and ketchup. Season with salt, black pepper and olive oil. Refrigerate overnight.
2. Take out of the refrigerator half an hour before serving.

Tabuleh

A tasty Arab salad made of bulgur wheat and fresh vegetables. Instant couscous (coarse grain) may be used instead of the bulgur.

Ingredients (serves 4)

1 cup coarsely ground bulgur wheat, soaked in water for 30 minutes and drained
2 cups fresh parsley, chopped
1 red onion, chopped
2 tomatoes, peeled and chopped (optional)
1 sweet green pepper, chopped

1-2 tablespoons lemon juice
3 tablespoons extra virgin olive oil
1 pinch ground allspice
1 pinch cinnamon
1 teaspoon sumac (optional)
Salt to taste
To Serve:
2/3 cup pomegranate seeds (optional)

Mix all the ingredients and set aside for 30 minutes to allow the flavors to settle (do not refrigerate). Add the pomegranate seeds, toss lightly and serve.

Spicy Moroccan Carrot Salad

The choice between piquant and tongue-scorching hot is all yours.

Ingredients (serves 6-8)

8-10 carrots, peeled
2 cloves garlic, crushed
1 teaspoon cayenne pepper
2 tablespoons freshly squeezed lemon juice

1 tablespoon oil
1 teaspoon salt
1/2 teaspoon ground cumin
Chopped parsley
1/2-2 teaspoons zhug or harissa (p. 298)

1. Cook the carrots in boiling water for about 30 minutes or until tender.
2. Allow to cool and slice into coins.
3. Mix the remaining ingredients, pour over the carrot slices and mix well. Let stand for a minimum of one hour.

Pickled Turnip and Beetroot

Ingredients (to fill a 1-liter/1-quart jar)

3-4 beetroots, peeled and sliced
4-5 turnips, peeled and sliced
1 teaspoon salt

1. Place the turnip slices on a kitchen towel for one hour and allow to dry.
2. Dissolve the salt in 3 cups of water.
3. Arrange the turnip slices in a jar, place the beetroots on top and pour the brine over everything. Close the lid tight and leave in a cool shaded place for one week.

Roasted Peppers in Marinade

Very popular and easy to make, this Balkan delicacy keeps well in the refrigerator and is used in many dishes. Use sweet red peppers. The long, pointed kapia variety is especially good, but ordinary ones will do.

Ingredients (serves 6)

12 kapia peppers or 6-8 regular sweet red peppers

2-3 tablespoons white wine vinegar

2 cloves garlic, chopped or sliced thinly

Salt

3 parsley and/or dill sprigs

1. Roast the peppers over an open flame or under the grill until the skin is charred.
2. Allow to cool, preferably in a sealed plastic bag to make peeling easier. Peel and remove the membranes and seeds. Chop the peppers coarsely, or cut into strips or large wedges.
3. Transfer the peppers to a bowl, add the vinegar, garlic, salt and parsley and/or dill. Refrigerate. After a few hours the peppers will absorb the marinade flavors and can be served. If you prefer a pronounced sour taste, marinate them for a few days. Remove from the refrigerator half an hour before serving.

Deep-Fried Cauliflower Florets

This is the easiest way to enjoy these tasty crisp florets. Use only super-fresh cauliflower for a crunchy effect. Tahini complements the taste beautifully.

Ingredients (serves 4-6)

1 small cauliflower, cut into florets
Oil for deep-frying
1/4 cup freshly squeezed lemon juice

3 tablespoons chopped fresh parsley
Salt
1/2 cup raw tahini

1. Heat the oil and deep-fry the cauliflower florets until golden brown. Transfer to a colander to drain and cool.
2. Put in a bowl and season with salt, lemon juice and chopped parsley.
3. Mix the tahini with 1/2 cup of water, some lemon juice and salt until it is smooth and creamy. Serve the cauliflower with tahini dip on the side or mix prior to serving.

Matboucha

Salata Matboucha is "cooked salad" in Arabic. It is a popular dish that tastes great hot or cold. It keeps well, even in the freezer, so preparing large quantities is a good idea.

Ingredients (makes about 1 kg/2 lb)

4-5 ripe tomatoes
4 sweet red peppers
4 hot green peppers
8-10 cloves garlic, crushed
1/2 cup oil

1 tablespoon paprika
1 teaspoon cayenne pepper
1 teaspoon salt
1 pinch sugar
1 tablespoon tomato paste

1. Using a sharp knife, cut a cross on the bottom of each tomato. Blanch the tomatoes briefly in boiling water, peel, halve, remove the seeds and chop coarsely.
2. Roast the red and green peppers over an open flame or under the grill. Allow to cool (preferably in a sealed plastic bag to make peeling easier), peel and remove the membranes and seeds. Chop coarsely.
3. Cook the tomatoes in a saucepan for 5-10 minutes, until all the liquid evaporates.
4. Add the remaining ingredients except the tomato paste. Lower the heat and cook for 2 hours, stirring occasionally.
5. Add the tomato paste and cook for another 30 minutes. The salad is ready when it is shiny and very thick. Keep in the refrigerator up to 10 days or in the freezer up to 3 months. Bring to room temperature before serving.

Israeli Meze

Erez Komarovsky, one of Israel's most original and creative chefs, offers his unique version of the Israeli meze. Fresh seasonal fruits and vegetables and quality olive oil are the stars of the table.

Grated Radish Salad

Ingredients (serves 4-6)

2-3 large radishes, peeled and grated
1/2 cup cracked green olives
Freshly ground white pepper to taste

1/4 cup freshly squeezed lemon juice
Coarse sea salt to taste
2-3 tablespoons aromatic olive oil

1. Mix the grated radish with the olives. Season liberally with the salt, white pepper and lemon juice and set aside to rest for 5 minutes.
2. Heap the salad on a serving plate. Pour the olive oil on top and allow it to drain and form small puddles on the bottom of the plate.

Hummus-style Bean Dip

Ingredients (serves 6)

1/2 kg (1 lb 2 oz) dry white beans, soaked in water overnight
1 cup raw tahini
1/2 cup freshly squeezed lemon juice
The sauce:
2 tablespoons honey
3 tablespoons pickled (Moroccan) lemons, chopped (p. 296)

10 fresh sage leaves, chopped
Salt
2 hot green peppers, roasted, peeled and chopped (see instructions on p. 54)
1/2 cup aromatic (Souri) olive oil
3-4 tablespoons garlic confit
To Serve:
1/2 cup roasted almonds

1. Drain the beans and cook in salted water for 3-4 hours, until completely soft.
2. Mash the beans in a wooden mortar and pestle (or in a food processor) with some of the cooking liquid. Add the tahini and lemon juice, season with salt and mix well.
3. Combine the sauce ingredients and adjust the seasoning.
4. Pour the sauce over the bean dip and top up with roasted almonds.

Serving Suggestion Ladle the bean dip over a bed of cooked beans (see photo opposite).

Garlic Confit

Put peeled cloves from 10 garlic heads in a small saucepan, add about 3/4 of a cup of olive oil (to cover) and 1 small chopped hot green pepper (optional). Bring to a simmer on a very low heat, remove from the stove and wait until the oil stops bubbling. Repeat the cycle 4 times. Bring to a boil a fifth time and let the garlic simmer in the oil for about 10 minutes until it turns golden. Store in oil in a sealed jar until needed. The confit will keep up to a year.

Fennel and Pistachio Salad

Ingredients (serves 4-6)

3-4 small fennel bulbs
1/2 cup filleted lemon segments (see instructions on p. 61)
Coarse sea salt
1/4 cup delicate olive oil

1 hot green pepper, chopped finely
2 tablespoons honey
1/2 cup pistachio nuts, roasted and crushed

1. Cut the fennel bulbs into thin longitudinal slices. Soak in ice water for about 30 minutes. Drain, mix the fennel slices with the lemon segments, sprinkle coarse sea salt on top and set aside to rest for 15 minutes.
2. Mix the fennel and lemon salad with the olive oil, hot pepper and honey. Sprinkle the roasted pistachio nuts on top and serve.

Beetroot and Pomegranate Salad

Ingredients (serves 6)

3-4 medium beetroots
2 tablespoons pomegranate concentrate
2-3 tablespoons freshly squeezed lemon juice
2-3 dried chili peppers, crushed

Coarse sea salt
1/4 cup delicate olive oil
1/2 cup fresh coriander leaves
1 cup pomegranate seeds

1. Boil the beetroots in water until tender. Cool, peel and cut into very small dice.
2. Mix with the pomegranate concentrate, lemon juice, peppers and coarse sea salt. Set aside for about 15 minutes.
3. Mix the salad with the coriander leaves and pomegranate seeds, pour the olive oil on top and serve.

Citrus Fillet Salad

Ingredients (serves 6)

4 oranges
2 red grapefruits
2 blood oranges
1/2 cup young garden cress, leaves only
1/3 cup olive oil

1-2 tablespoons silan (date honey)
or 1 tablespoon honey
Coarse sea salt
1 hot red pepper, seeded and chopped

1. Fillet all citrus fruit: Cut off the top and the base of the fruit to make it more stable. Place on the work surface and cut off the skin, including the white pulp. Hold the fruit in one hand and, using a knife, separate the fillets between the membranes.
2. Transfer the fillets to a bowl and mix them with the hot red pepper. Add the silan (or honey), olive oil and garden cress leaves and season with coarse sea salt. Toss gently and serve.

Celery and Kashkaval Cheese Salad

Ingredients (serves 4-6)

1 bunch celery (one with young, light-colored stalks)
Freshly squeezed juice of 2 lemons
Coarse sea salt
10 top-quality anchovy fillets, diced

1/4-1/3 cup olive oil
100 g (31/2 oz) ripe kashkaval or
Parmesan cheese
Coarsely ground white pepper

1. Discard the coarse outer stalks of the celery bunch and cut the inner stalks into thin strips. A vegetable peeler can be used to shave the stalks lengthwise.
2. Mix the celery strips with the lemon juice and some salt. Be careful with the salt — both the cheese and the anchovies are salty!
3. Mix the anchovy fillets with the olive oil and add to the celery strips.
4. Using the finest grater, grate the cheese over the salad, sprinkle some ground white pepper on top and serve immediately.

The Israeli Breakfast

Top to bottom: **Pina ba Rosh,** in the hilltop town of Rosh Pina — a rustic breakfast with a view. **Café Benedict** in Tel Aviv — a variety of breakfast menus are offered throughout the day. Breakfast buffet in **Mitzpeh Hayamim,** spa-hotel near Safed — almost all of the items on the menu are produced or grown on the premises. Opposite: **Lechem Erez, Herzliya:** a huge slice of toasted bread serves as a plate for the omelet with labane cheese and marinated peppers.

No one who has stayed at a hotel in Israel will forget the sumptuous Israeli breakfast. The origin of this unique phenomenon is proletarian: kibbutz workers, who began their day in the fields before dawn and were ravenous by 7 AM, gathered in the communal dining room for a hearty breakfast of whatever fresh produce was on hand. They helped themselves to vegetables (which they cut up to make a salad), freshly squeezed orange juice, eggs, milk and dairy products laid out rather unceremoniously on a bare table.

Fresh farm produce was scarce in the early years of the State of Israel and items like eggs and fresh meat were practically nonexistent in the cities. Back in the 1950s, city folk could savor the wonders of the kibbutz breakfast only if they had the good fortune to spend a vacation at one of the kibbutz guest houses — a privilege reserved for employees of government companies and Histadrut (trade union) institutions.

When the first luxury hotels opened in the 1950s, they adopted the kibbutz breakfast and turned it into a lavish buffet. The culinary logic was simple: since these establishments adhered to the laws of kashrut prohibiting serving meat and dairy together, chefs had to come up with a menu to compensate non-Jewish tourists for the absence of their customary breakfast foods. The result was a dairy buffet that showcased the best of local produce. A typical five-star breakfast buffet will display an abundance of fresh vegetables and fruit, a battery of salads, cheese platters, soft cheeses and cheese dips, marinated fish, several kinds of olives, eggs cooked to order, pancakes, fresh fruit juices, quiches, pies, freshly baked breads and rolls, croissants and Danish pastry, yogurt (plain, low-fat and fruit), sour cream, butter, jams, marmalades and preserves, cakes, special dishes for children, and much more. On Saturday mornings, when cooking is forbidden, Yemenite-style *jakhnun* (fat-laden pastry baked overnight), bourekas and quiches are served instead of omelets.

Hotels are not the only place to enjoy this morning treat. Most cafés and restaurants offer a variety of breakfast menus (the latest trend is to serve them throughout the day). The most original and probably most delicious breakfast can be found at a country inn, known locally as a zimmer (room in German). Based almost entirely on homemade products, breakfast is the pride and joy of these family establishments, most of them situated in scenic northern Israel. Breads, fruit preserves and cheeses are made on the premises, and fresh fruits and vegetables are picked daily from the garden.

the street and the market

Open Air Markets

Israel is part of the Middle East, and in the Middle East the open-air market, also known as the souk, is one of the most popular forms of commerce. Even today when supermarkets are preferred for everyday shopping, the souk retains its charm and attracts both shoppers and sightseers.

The open-air markets are first and foremost food markets. As such, they are intimately tied to local cuisine. Housewives, chefs and restaurant owners, locals and tourists all flock to the stands in search of fresh produce and other food products. As markets evolve into tourist attractions, many stands are adding ready-to-eat street food to their usual offerings, giving visitors a taste of the local fare.

Produce is fresh and accessible and you can touch and select fruits and vegetables at your leisure. Butchers offer freshly-slaughtered chickens, complete with feet, feathers and cockscombs. Fishmongers will net the carp you point to in a tank, and gut and clean it for you. Prices are negotiable and haggling is the norm. Vendors often employ funny songs and other theatrics to promote their goods. The atmosphere is dense, casually familiar, cheerful and noisy, with added urgency as the weekend draws near.

Most markets are permanent and offer a wide range of goods: from fresh produce to illegally-copied DVDs, from inexpensive textiles to fresh fish and poultry, from household goods to flowers, from wallets to freshly baked breads.

The two most picturesque general markets are the Carmel Market in Tel Aviv (founded in 1927) and Mahane-Yehuda in Jerusalem (founded in 1928). Both are primarily food markets with the emphasis on fresh produce, and yet each reflects the unique character of its city. The clientele of the Carmel Market is a heady mix of sophisticated urban types, foreign workers (mainly from Southeast Asia), new immigrants (mostly from the former Soviet Union), and inhabitants of the neighboring Yemenite Quarter. The offerings range,

accordingly, from budget clothes to organic herbs, from boutique cheeses to exotic products from the Far East.

Mahane-Yehuda is Jerusalem to the core. Shoppers and vendors have known each other for years. There are fewer stalls with trendy fancy vegetables and a larger range of authentic *balladi* produce. Most of the shoppers are housewives, mainly Sephardic, and the vast majority of the goods are strictly kosher.

Other prominent food markets are the Hatikva Market in south Tel Aviv, the Bukharian Market in Jerusalem, the markets in Netanya, Hadera, Rosh-Ha'ayin and Haifa, and the Bedouin Market in Be'er-Sheva. When visiting northern Israel you shouldn't miss souks in Nazareth and Old Acre, both brimming with exotic goods and flavors of the Middle East. And of course there is the Old City of Jerusalem with its huge rambling bazaar that covers a sizable portion of the ancient quarters. One can easily get lost in its winding alleys — the scenery, the atmosphere and the goods change as you move from the butchers market to the perfumes, the goldsmiths, the leather workers, the food.

Another souk worth visiting is the Lewinski Market in south Tel Aviv. No longer confined to its original building, it has spilled over into nearby streets with exotic spices, dried fruits, legumes, nuts, rice and pasta, smoked, pickled and dried fish, olives, pickles, oils, and ethnic pastries. Foodies and chefs come here to buy Greek olives, real lakerda (Turkish pickled fish), dried Persian lemons and rare condiments.

Finally, there are the roving markets that operate at a different venue each day of the week. A prominent example is the Ramla-Lod market. Once a popular local market in Ramla, it can now be found at a different announced location each weekday. A lovely market operates on weekends in Ma'alot Tarshicha in the Western Galilee, amicably shared by Arab and Jewish vendors and farmers.

Prices are negotiable and haggling is the norm. Vendors often employ funny songs and other theatrics to promote their goods. The atmosphere is dense, casually familiar, cheerful and noisy, with added urgency as the weekend draws near.

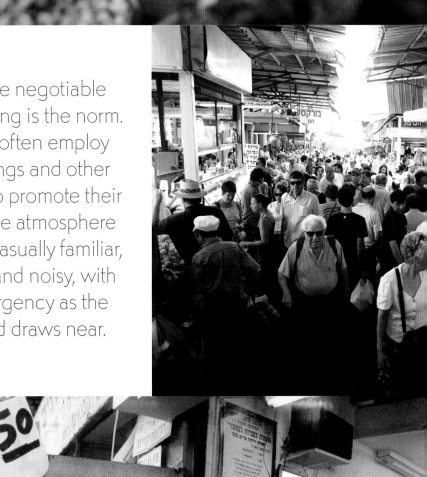

Falafel

Falafel, a common Middle Eastern street food, is synonymous with Israeli cuisine and Israel in general. It is made from mashed broad (fava) beans or chickpeas, the latter being the most popular locally. Every city, town and neighborhood has a favorite falafel establishment, sporting such names as The Falafel King, The Real Falafel King, The New Falafel King, The King of All Kings, The Falafel Queen, The Desperate Man's Falafel, or simply Nissim's Falafel, Zvika's Falafel or Falafel for the Young. Travelers make it a point to call at the falafel stand reputed to be the best in town to sample the local product and compare it with their hometown version. Falafel vendors come up with all sorts of gimmicks to set their stand apart from the competition. They invent special extras (like deep-fried, battered potato slices or pita wedges), offer an abundance of free salads and pickles for the price of a single portion of falafel, and perform juggling acts as they make the falafel balls.

With the introduction of American-style fast food in the 1980s, falafel gradually lost its supremacy as Israel's most popular street food. It is making a comeback today in traditional as well as yuppie versions.

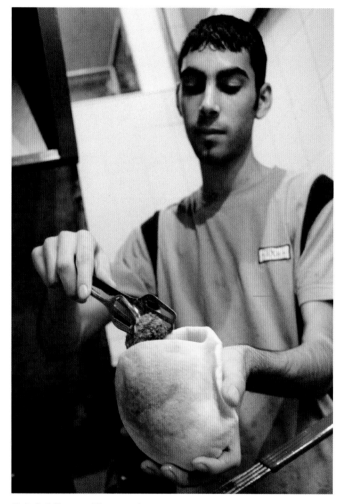

Falafel Diana, Nazareth
Though not as famous as the mother restaurant of the same name just across the street (p. 172), this falafel joint is considered to be one of the best in town.

Falafel — Basic Recipe

To make perfect falafels it is best to use a special tool, but a small ice cream scoop will do just as well. You can also use wet hands. The classic way to serve falafel is, of course, in a pita, but it is equally good on a bed of thick yogurt or labane (p. 269), or as a crunchy addition to a plate of hummus (p. 47).

Ingredients (makes 10-12 generous servings)

1 kg (2 lb 4 oz) dry chickpeas soaked in water overnight
1 large onion
2/3 cup garlic cloves, peeled
1/2 cup fresh parsley, coarsely chopped
1/2 cup fresh coriander, coarsely chopped
1 teaspoon toasted coriander seeds
5-6 Shipka peppers (small hot green pickled peppers) or 1/2-1 teaspoon dried hot red pepper
11/4 tablespoons ground cumin
Pinch of ground cardamom

1 tablespoon salt
1 teaspoon freshly ground black pepper
1 level teaspoon baking powder
2 tablespoons flour
1 level tablespoon baking soda
4-5 tablespoons water
Oil for deep-frying
To Serve:
Oven-fresh pita
Tahini dip (p. 38)
Hummus dip (p. 47)
Vegetable salad (p. 22)

1. Drain the soaked chickpeas and rinse thoroughly. Grind them with the onion, garlic, parsley, coriander and Shipka peppers (or the dry hot red pepper) in a meat grinder or food processor, but do not purée; a slightly coarse consistency makes crunchier falafels. Season with cumin, cardamom, salt and black pepper. Add the baking powder and flour, mix well and refrigerate for one hour.
2. Before frying, dissolve the baking soda in 4-5 tablespoons water, add to the batter and mix well.
3. Moisten a falafel tool or ice cream scoop and form falafel patties, or roll walnut-size balls with moist hands.
4. Heat the oil for deep-frying to medium heat. Oil that is too hot will brown the falafels on the outside and leave the inside uncooked. Check the temperature by test-frying one ball. Fry in small batches on both sides, 4-5 minutes, until the balls turn golden-brown. Remove with a slotted spoon and drain the excess oil in a colander.
5. Serve promptly in a pita, spread with hummus dip. Add some vegetable salad and drip tahini on top.

Green Falafel Add one more cup of chopped parsley and coriander and grind with the rest of the ingredients.
Red Falafel Add 3 tablespoons of filfel chuma (p. 296) to the other spices.
Yellow Falafel Add 1 teaspoon ground turmeric to the other spices.
Extra-crunchy Falafel Dip the balls in sesame seeds before frying.

Fish Falafel in Spicy Harissa Mayonnaise

Avi Steinitz, Avenue Convention Center, Airport City

Halfway between fish cakes and a traditional falafel, this dish takes the best from both worlds: the tender taste of fish and the nutty crunchiness of fried chickpeas. Serve in a pita, as you would a falafel, or as a starter or cocktail snack with fresh yogurt or a spicy sauce.

Ingredients (serves 12)

200 g (7 oz) dry chickpeas, soaked in water overnight
900 g (2 lb) fresh skinned saltwater fish fillets (grouper, sea bream or similar)
3-4 onions, quartered
7 stalks parsley, coarsely chopped
3 stalks coriander, coarsely chopped
3 cloves garlic, peeled
60 g (2 oz) sesame seeds

Oil for deep-frying
Harissa Mayonnaise:
1/2 cup mayonnaise
1 teaspoon (or more) harissa (p. 298)
2 cloves garlic, crushed
1-2 tablespoons freshly squeezed lemon juice
Salt to taste

1. Drain the chickpeas and rinse thoroughly. Put in a pan, cover with plenty of water and cook for at least 2 hours until soft.
2. Grind the chickpeas with the fish, herbs, onions and garlic in a meat grinder. If you use a food processor, work in short pulses in order not to mash the delicate flesh of the fish.
3. Add the spices and sesame seeds and mix well. Refrigerate for half an hour.
4. Moisten a falafel tool or ice cream scoop and form the falafel patties, or wet your hands and make small walnut-size balls.
5. Heat oil for deep-frying to medium heat (150°C/300°F). Fry in small batches on both sides for 3 minutes until the falafels turn golden-brown. Remove with a slotted spoon and drain the excess oil in a colander.
6. Mix the ingredients for harissa mayonnaise and serve alongside the falafels.

Shawarma

Traditionally, shawarma (from çevirme in Turkish, meaning "rotating", and also known as döner kebab) is made from lamb. In practice, Israeli shawarma is usually made from turkey with lamb fat added. To make the real thing one needs a huge skewer fitted with a special heating device. Sliced marinated meat is stacked on the skewer, which rotates slowly and roasts it on all sides. The meat is then shaved and stuffed into a pita together with. . . . here the argument begins. The purists insist that all a good shawarma needs is hummus or tahini dip and parsley sprigs. Others like their shawarma with all the trimmings: fresh or fried onion rings, French fries, salad, pickles and tahini.

Homemade Shawarma

The process is very different from traditional shawarma, but the result is quite similar, and extremely tasty. Deboned chicken thighs are baked in the oven and stir-fried prior to serving. Extended marinating in a massive amount of spices gives the chicken fantastic flavors and a tantalizing color. While you're at it, prepare a double quantity of the seasoning mix and keep in the freezer. This recipe was developed by a talented amateur cook, Israel Scherrer.

Shawarma Shemesh, Ramat Gan
One of the best shawarma spots in the greater Tel Aviv area.

Ingredients (serves 8-10)
11/2 kg (3 lb 5 oz) deboned chicken thighs
The Marinade:
3/4 cup olive oil
2 tablespoons curry powder
1 tablespoon garam masala (Indian seasoning mix, available in spice shops)
1 tablespoon chicken soup mix
For Frying:
3 tablespoons oil
3 onions, sliced
Salt and freshly ground black pepper

1. Mix the marinade ingredients in a disposable baking dish (the most practical because the process is messy). Add the chicken and mix well. Marinate for a minimum of 5 hours (or overnight) in the refrigerator.
2. Preheat the oven to 200°C (400°F).
3. Bake for 45 minutes. The entire process up to this point may be completed a day or two ahead and the baked chicken stored in the refrigerator.
4. Before serving, finely slice the chunks of chicken.
5. Fry the onion in oil until golden and remove from the pan.
6. Add the chicken with some of the marinade to the pan. Season and stir-fry for a few minutes, until the edges are golden-brown. Spread the fried onions over the meat and serve.

Laffa "Lilit"

Omer ben Gal, Lilit Restaurant, Tel Aviv

This up-market version of schawarma is a flatbread sandwich with stir-fried steak strips, flame-roasted eggplants and two tasty salads.

Ingredients (serves 4)

The Eggplants:
2 eggplants
1/2 cup olive oil
Juice of 1-2 lemons
Coarse salt and crushed black pepper

The Matboucha Salad:
4 ripe tomatoes
1 hot green pepper
Pinch of sugar
Pinch of salt
1/4 cup olive oil

The Hyssop Salad:
1/2 cup fresh hyssop (or oregano) leaves
1 onion, thinly sliced

1 tablespoon sumac
1/4 cup olive oil
1/4 cup freshly squeezed lemon juice
Salt and freshly ground black pepper

The Steak Sandwich:
Olive oil for brushing
1 laffa (Iraqi flatbread, p. 86) quartered, or
2 pita breads, each halved into two disks
1 kg (2 lb 4 oz) beef sirloin, tenderloin or
entrecote, cut into thin slices

To Serve:
1 cup thick tahini dip (p. 38)

1. **Prepare the eggplants:** Flame roast the eggplants (see instructions on p. 31). Cool slightly, scoop out the flesh, chop and mix with olive oil, lemon juice and salt. Set aside.

2. **Prepare the matboucha salad:** Preheat oven to maximum temperature.

3. Brush the tomatoes and the pepper with olive oil, season with salt and sugar and bake for 15 minutes. Take out the pepper and continue baking the tomatoes for another 5 minutes until they become dark brown.

4. In a deep bowl, mash the grilled tomatoes with a fork, season with olive oil and salt.

5. Seed and chop the pepper and add to the tomatoes. Keep warm.

6. **Prepare the hyssop salad:** Mix all the ingredients and set aside.

7. **Assemble the sandwich:** Brush the laffa quarters or pita halves with olive oil and toast under the oven broiler or on a barbecue grill for a few minutes. Transfer to a serving plate. Spread the tahini dip on the toasted bread and spoon on some of the matboucha and chopped eggplant.

8. Heat a large skillet over a high heat. Brush the meat with olive oil, season with salt and pepper and stir-fry for a couple of minutes.

9. Place the meat on top of the matboucha salad and eggplant, heap on some of the hyssop salad, sprinkle olive oil and serve with tahini dip on the side.

Shakshuka

Shakshuka is one of those dishes you can make even when your refrigerator appears to be empty. Now enjoyed all day long, this dish of Lybian origin began as a sumptuous workingman's dawn-till-noon meal. It has three mandatory ingredients: tomatoes, hot sauce and eggs. Anything else is open for debate, Israeli style. The most popular ingredients are onions, red peppers, leeks, potatoes, sausages and kernel corn. Served in the same frying pan it is cooked in, with coarsely sliced, soft white bread and a salad, shakshuka makes for a hearty meal. Extra bread is always welcome to mop up the sauce.

Tips For Perfect Shakshuka

Cooking Utensil Use a heavy deep skillet or a large shallow saucepan. Make sure the lid has a valve to provide an outlet for the steam.

Tomatoes Shakshuka devotées insist on fresh tomatoes for the sauce, but canned tomatoes (crushed or diced) and tomato paste are just as good.

Spices Filfel chuma (a North African hot sauce containing garlic, paprika and hot peppers) is the preferred seasoning, but cayenne pepper, Yemenite zhug or harissa may be used as well. In any case — the sauce must be very spicy!

Important! Make sure the tomato sauce is cooked and fully seasoned before you add the eggs. Once they're in the pan you can't stir the sauce or adjust the seasoning.

Handling the Eggs The objective here is perfect, unbroken poached eggs topping the tomato sauce. To prevent broken yolks, carefully break each egg into a bowl and slide it onto the tomato sauce. If you are cooking a mega-shakshuka, use a wooden spoon to make small wells in the sauce and pour one egg into each one to ensure everybody gets a fair share.

Doctor Shakshuka, Jaffa

This bustling cavernous restaurant filled with items from the nearby flea market is popular with locals and tourists alike. Spicy shakshuka served in a skillet is the signature dish, but couscous, mafroum and chreime are also worth trying.

Shakshuka — Basic Recipe

This is the basic version found in most workers' kitchens. See more elaborate versions below.

Ingredients (serves 4)

4 tablespoons oil, for frying
2 cloves garlic, crushed
5 large tomatoes, peeled and diced (or
11/2 cups canned tomatoes, crushed
1 tablespoon zhug (p. 298), filfel chuma
(p. 296) or harissa (p. 298) or a mixture of
crushed garlic, paprika and hot peppers

Salt and freshly ground black pepper to
taste
1/2 teaspoon ground cumin (optional)
Pinch of ground caraway (optional)
2 tablespoons tomato paste
8 eggs

1. Heat the oil in a large deep skillet and lightly fry the garlic. Add the tomatoes and seasonings and cook for 15-20 minutes over low heat, partly covered.
2. Add the tomato paste, cover and simmer for a few more minutes. Adjust the seasoning — the sauce should have a strong, piquant flavor.
3. Break the eggs one by one and slide onto the tomato sauce, arranging the yolks around the pan.
4. Turn heat to low and cook until the egg whites set (about 5-7 minutes). Partly cover the pan to prevent the sauce from spraying around the kitchen. Cover completely if you like your eggs "over hard".

Shakshuka with Onions and Peppers Slice one onion and two sweet red peppers and fry lightly. Add the garlic and tomatoes and continue according to the basic recipe.

Shakshuka with Sausages Lightly fry sliced merguez sausages or small cocktail sausages, or grill the sausages first and then add them to the pan. Add the garlic and tomatoes and continue according to the basic recipe.

Israeli Army Shakshuka This version utilizes two canned staples usually found in army kitchens and combat rations: kernel corn and baked beans. Lightly fry diced onions, peppers, garlic and sausages. Add the drained kernel corn, the baked beans and the tomatoes and continue according to the basic recipe.

Shakshuka with Spinach and Feta
Shir Halpern, Food Writer

A mild version of shakshuka without tomato sauce

Ingredients (serves 4)
2 leeks (white part only), finely sliced
1 tablespoon butter
500 g (1 lb 2 oz) fresh spinach leaves,
washed and trimmed

2 cloves garlic, crushed
Salt and freshly ground black pepper
6 eggs
100 g (4 oz) feta cheese, crumbled

1. Melt the butter in a large deep skillet and sauté the leeks until soft and translucent but not brown.
2. Add spinach and garlic and sauté for 5 minutes. Season gently — remember that the cheese is quite salty.
3. Break the eggs one by one and slide onto the spinach. Arrange the yolks around the pan. Sprinkle the cheese around the pan.
4. Turn heat to low, cover the pan and simmer until the egg whites set, 5-7 minutes. Serve immediately.

Chili Shakshuka
Shir Halpern, Food Writer

The combination of peppers (sweet and hot) and fresh coriander gives the shakshuka a Mexican twist. Serve with hot tortillas instead of bread.

Ingredients (serves 4)
3 sweet peppers (red, green and yellow),
seeded and sliced into thin strips
1 tablespoon olive oil
2 cloves garlic, crushed

1 hot green pepper, seeded and finely chopped
Salt and freshly ground black pepper
6 eggs
1/2 cup fresh coriander, chopped

1. Heat the oil in a deep skillet and stir-fry the sweet peppers over medium heat for 5 minutes. Add the garlic and the hot green pepper and fry for another 5 minutes. Season to taste.
2. Break the eggs one by one and slide onto the peppers. Arrange the yolks around the pan.
3. Turn heat to low, partly cover the pan and simmer until the egg whites set, 5-7 minutes. Sprinkle with chopped coriander and serve immediately.

Pita, Laffa and Lahukh

Pita is not just an extremely popular pocket bread, it is the mainstay of the way Israelis eat. Anything can go into a pita — from chocolate spread (a favorite school snack) to a whole lunch, such as schnitzel with salad and French fries. Apart from packing it with innumerable foodstuffs, pita has another important use: to mop up hummus, tahini, labane, eggplant and other dips, spreads and salads. Pita must be oven-fresh or it's no good. Try the following recipe for your own version of this wonderful pocket-bread, followed by laffa, a large soft flatbread (the local answer to tortilla), and lahukh, fluffy Yemenite pan-fried bread.

Pita

Ingredients (for 10 pitas)

500 g (1 lb 2 oz, 31/2 cups) bread flour
25 g (1 oz) fresh yeast
360 ml (121/2 oz, 11/2 cups) water

1 tablespoon sugar
1/2 tablespoon salt
30 ml (1 fl oz, 2 tablespoons) olive oil

1. Mix the yeast with the flour in a mixer fitted with a kneading hook. Add the water, sugar, salt and olive oil and knead for 10 minutes, until the dough is smooth, shiny and slightly sticky.
2. Transfer the dough to a large greased bowl. Sprinkle olive oil over it, cover with cling wrap and allow to rise to twice its original size.
3. Preheat the oven to maximum (250°C/500°F).
4. Place the dough on a work surface sprinkled with flour and divide into 10 equal parts. Roll each part into a ball. Cover with a moist towel and leave for 10 minutes.
5. Roll out each ball into a disk 10-12 cm (4 inches) in diameter and 1/2 cm (1/4 inch) thick. Arrange on a tray lined with baking paper and bake for 5 minutes, just until the pitas swell up and begin to show golden spots. Avoid over-baking, which will cause them to dry up.
6. Remove from the oven and allow to cool slightly. Cover the pitas with a kitchen towel for a few minutes to keep them soft.

Pita with Sesame and Nigella Seeds Toss the dough balls in a bowl containing 1/2 cup sesame seeds and 1 tablespoon nigella seeds, until fully coated. Roll into disks (the seeds will sink into the dough) and bake as instructed.
Pita with Za'atar Combine 1/2 cup za'atar spice mix (p. 299) with 1/2 cup olive oil, coarse salt to taste and a few drops of lemon juice, until a spread-like paste forms. Spread a tablespoon of the paste on each pita just before placing in an oven preheated to 200°C (400°F). Bake for 10 minutes. The heavy coating and relatively low baking temperature produce a thicker flat pita with no air pocket.

Laffa (Iraqi Pita)

A huge, thin, very soft flatbread

Ingredients (for 6 laffas)
See the basic recipe for pita (p. 84)

1. Follow the basic recipe for pita, but divide the dough into 6 equal parts. Allow to rest for 10 minutes.
2. Roll out each part into 30-35 cm (12-14 inch) diameter disks and bake for 10 minutes at 180°C (350°F).
3. Remove from the oven and cover immediately with a kitchen towel. Leave for a few minutes until the laffa loses its crispness and becomes soft and flexible.

Stove-top Laffa Preheat a wok or a large, flat frying pan placed upside-down on the stove (or over a campfire). Toast the dough disks, one by one, without oil, directly on the dry wok or pan. Turn over when brown scorch marks appear here and there and toast for another minute. Stack the laffas on a large plate or tray covered with a towel to keep them soft.

Lahukh — Yemenite Flatbread

This fluffy, delicate pan-fried bread is so good you are in danger of finishing it before the guests arrive. When frying lahukh, the pan must be allowed to cool between rounds so the bottom part of the lahukh remains smooth, without bubble holes. To cool down the pan, dip it in a large bowl of ice water or hold upside-down under a running tap.

Ingredients (for 20 lahukh breads)

500 g (1 lb 2 oz, 31/2 cups) flour
25 g (1 oz) fresh yeast
1 level tablespoon salt

1/2 tablespoon sugar
3 slices white bread
Oil for frying

1. Put the flour, yeast, salt and sugar in a deep bowl and mix with 3 cups of water to form a batter.
2. Soak the bread slices in water for 5 minutes, remove, squeeze off the excess water and mash in a blender. Add to the batter and mix well.
3. Cover the bowl, leave at room temperature for about two hours to allow the batter to rise to twice its original size.
4. Heat a non-stick pan and oil it lightly. Wipe excess oil with a paper towel — no further oiling will be required during frying. Ladle a portion of the batter into the pan. Fry on medium heat until the top of the lahukh fills with bubbles and the bottom turns dark brown. Do not fry on the other side. Cover with a towel to prevent drying and serve warm.

Jerusalem Mixed Grill

Jerusalem's best-loved street food and once most closely-guarded secret. The credit for this concotion goes to the now extinct Stekiyat Makam, a hole-in-the-wall in the Mahane-Yehuda Market that was a popular spot in the early seventies. The story goes that a group of hungry soldiers were clamoring for service when the kitchen was almost out of meat. So the grillman stir-fried some chicken offals and onions on the hot griddle, spiced it all up and served it to the impatient crowd. The rest is history.

Jerusalem Mixed Grill — Home Version

Ingredients (serves 6)

250 g (9 oz) chicken livers, diced
200 g (7 oz) chicken spleens, cleaned and halved
250 g (9 oz) chicken hearts
1 whole chicken breast, diced
4 onions, sliced
1 teaspoon baharat spice mix (p. 299)
1 teaspoon paprika

Salt
1/2 cup olive oil
To Serve:
Pita breads
Pickled cucumbers, sliced
Shipka peppers (small, hot, pickled green peppers)
Tahini dip (p. 38)

1. Mix the various meats with the onions, spices and oil. Leave in the refrigerator for a minimum of 5 hours, up to 24 hours, or freeze in portions.
2. Heat a non-stick frying pan. Add the seasoned mix and stir-fry for 12-15 minutes until the meat is done.
3. Stuff in a pita and serve with pickles and a dollop of tahini dip.

Stekiyat Hatzot, Jerusalem
Literally "Midnight Steak House", this is
one of the most famous places in the
city to savor Jerusalem mixed grill. The
place is open during the day, but is at its
best in the evening hours, especially on
Thursday night when hundreds of taxi
drivers stop by for a weekly fix of their
favorite pita combo.

Jerusalem Bagel

According to popular belief, the Jerusalem bagel gained prominence after the Six Day War when Israelis began flocking to the Old City. There they discovered these chewy, sweetish bagels, accompanied by the ever-present mixture of hyssop and salt (*za'atar*) tucked into a piece of newspaper. Later on they became a favorite of football crowds at the Saturday matches. Nowadays these bagels are available everywhere, even in five-star hotels, but the original recipe remains a closely guarded secret. Jerusalem bagels are made from basic bread dough with extra oil and sugar but no salt. In this version, powdered milk is added to give the bagel its unique soft texture.

Making ahead

These soft bagels are best enjoyed oven fresh. If you want to save them for later, seal them in a plastic bag as soon as they have cooled off and freeze promptly. Defrost to room temperature and heat up for a few minutes in an oven preheated to 180°C (350°F).

Jerusalem Bagel — Home Version

Ingredients (makes 6 large bagels)

The Dough:
600 g (1 lb 5 oz, 4¼ cups) bread flour
20 g (¾ oz) fresh yeast
45 g (1½ oz, 3 tablespoons) sugar
60 ml (2 fl oz, ¼ cup) oil
2 heaping tablespoons powdered milk
360 ml (12½ fl oz, 1½ cups) lukewarm water

The Coating:
1 egg, beaten
1 cup sesame seeds mixed with
2 tablespoons sugar
To Serve:
Za'atar spice mix (p. 299)

1. In a mixer fitted with a kneading hook knead all the ingredients for the dough for 10 minutes to obtain a smooth, slightly sticky dough.
2. Transfer the dough to a bowl, cover and allow to rise to twice the original size.
3. Place the dough on a work surface sprinkled with flour and divide into 6 equal parts. Roll each part into a 50-cm (1·1/2-ft) sausage. Bring the ends together to make large elliptical bagels.
4. Arrange on a tray lined with baking paper, adequately spaced, brush with beaten egg, sprinkle with sesame and sugar mixture, cover and allow to rise to twice the original size.
5. Preheat the oven to 180°C (350°F) and bake the bagels for 15 minutes, or until they are golden with a dark brown underside.
6. Remove from the oven and allow to cool slightly. For extra-soft bagels, cover with a kitchen towel until they cool down. Serve warm with the za'atar mix.

Bourekas

Golden, warm, flaky and sinfully rich, bourekas are among the best-loved local snacks. Basically a breakfast or lunch food, fancy varieties are served even at the most elegant functions. The generic name bourekas, the plural of bourek, applies to an extensive family of savory pastry-based specialties originating in the Balkans. Always consumed with a guilty conscience because of their sky-high calorie count, they come in a variety of shapes, sizes and fillings, the most popular being cheese, mashed potatoes and spinach. Other fillings include eggplant, mushrooms, fried onions, and combinations of the above. Modern yuppie versions include pumpkin, tuna fish, sprouts and even tofu.

Bourekas are made from various types of dough including short pastry, puff pastry, phyllo and phyllas (a paper-thin variation of puff pastry), and shaped into rectangles, helixes, triangles and crescents. The crescent shape is normally reserved for the smaller short pastry variety called bourekitas. The highly-regarded Turkish-style bourekas are made from phyllo dough, baked on large trays, and cut to portions on order.

Bourekas are everywhere. They are sold from street stalls and baked on the premises in supermarkets. Bakeries often doubling as modest coffee shops offer them for breakfast with a hard-boiled egg, grated or sliced tomatoes, and a glass of chilled yogurt or Ayran, a yogurt-based drink of Turkish origin. And, of course, they can be made at home so you can enjoy them crisp and warm — the only proper way to savor this delight.

This Bourekas Cart is one of the landmarks of the Tel Aviv Carmel Market. Freshly made phyllo dough bourekas are stuffed with sliced tomatoes and hard-boiled eggs and served with pickled cucumbers.

Cheese Bourekas

Crisp, golden pastry triangles filled with cheese — a Balkan classic

Ingredients (makes 20 large bourekas)

The Cheese Filling:
500 g (1 lb 2 oz) *gvina levana* (fresh white cheese) or ricotta (5% fat)
250 g (9 oz) kashkaval or Parmesan cheese, grated
250 g (9 oz) brinza or feta cheese, crumbled
2 egg yolks
1 tablespoon corn starch
Freshly ground black pepper

The Pastry:
11/2 kg (3 lb 5 oz) puff pastry dough,
1 egg, beaten with 1 tablespoon water, for brushing
Sesame seeds for garnishing

1. Preheat the oven to 180°C (350°F).
2. Beat all the ingredients for the filling until smooth.
3. Roll the dough into a 1/2 cm (1/4 inch) thick sheet. Cut into 12-cm (5-inch) squares. Put one tablespoon of the filling in the center of each square, fold diagonally to form a triangle and pinch the edges together. Arrange the bourekas with sufficient space between them on a tray lined with baking paper.
4. Brush the triangles with the beaten egg and sprinkle sesame seeds on top.
5. Bake for about 30 minutes until the bourekas are golden and plump and smell delicious.

Potato Bourekas Boil 3 large potatoes until soft. Cool slightly, peel and mash. Fry 2 sliced onions in 3 tablespoons oil until golden. Cool slightly and add to the mashed potatoes. Mix with 1 beaten egg and season with salt and black pepper. You can also add 1/2 cup chopped parsley. Stuff and bake as described above.
Spinach and Cheese Bourekas Follow the recipe for spinach and cheese filling (Chukor) on p. 97.

Bourekas Sandwich
Open up freshly baked bourekas and stuff with a couple slices of hard-boiled eggs. You may also add pickled cucumbers and fresh tomatoes.

Eggplant and Cheese Bourekitas

The secret to this exquisite snack is its simplicity: the pastry is delicately crisp and the filling is very lightly seasoned. Don't be tempted to add spices. The flame-roasted eggplants combined with cheese need no enhancement.

Ingredients (makes 50 bourekitas)

The Pastry:
480 ml (17 fl oz, 2 cups) oil
240 ml (8 1/2 fl oz, 1 cup) water
1/2 teaspoon salt
1 kg (2 lb 4 oz, 7 cups) flour
The Filling:
5 eggplants

80 ml (3 fl oz, 1/3 cup) oil
300 g (10 1/2 oz) brinza or feta cheese, crumbled
The Coating:
1 egg, beaten
2/3 cup kashkaval or Parmesan cheese, grated, or sesame seeds

1. **Prepare the pastry:** Pour the oil, water and salt into a large bowl. Gradually add the flour and knead into a soft, non-sticky dough.
2. **Prepare the filling:** Roast the eggplants (see instructions on p. 31), peel and chop them, and drain in a colander for about 30 minutes.
3. Add the oil to the eggplants and mix well. Stir in the cheese.
4. **Prepare the bourekitas:** Preheat the oven to 200°C (400°F).
5. Form about 50 dough balls the size of large apricots and roll them into 1/2 cm (1/4 inch) thick disks. Put a spoonful of the filling in the center of each disk, fold into a crescent and pinch the edges to seal.
6. Arrange the bourekitas with sufficient space between them on a tray lined with baking paper. Brush with beaten egg and sprinkle grated cheese or sesame seeds on top. Bake for 20-25 minutes until golden.

Leon Bakery, Jaffa

One of the last remaining bakeries that produces handmade phyllo dough. A small ball of dough turns in a matter of minutes into a huge, almost transparent paper-thin sheet.

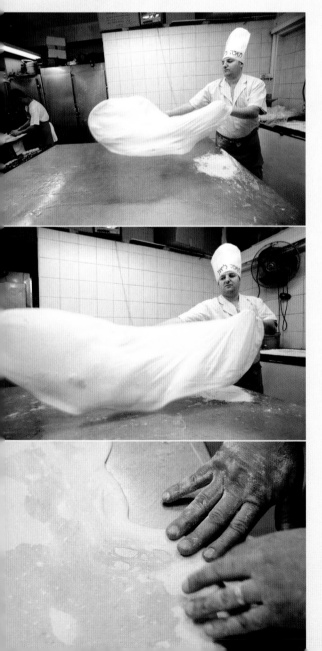

Chukor — Phyllo Spinach and Cheese Bourekas

These Turkish-style bourekas are similar to the ones bought at street stalls. Serve warm with pickles, olives, fresh vegetables and a hard-boiled egg.

Ingredients (makes 12 bourekas)

The Pastry:
12 sheets phyllo dough, defrosted overnight in the refrigerator
Olive oil for brushing

The Filling:
1 kg (2 lb 4 oz) fresh spinach leaves, washed, trimmed and chopped
450 g (1 lb) brinza or feta cheese, crumbled

100 g (31/2 oz) kashkaval or Parmesan cheese, grated
1 egg, beaten
Pinch of nutmeg
1 tablespoon breadcrumbs
Freshly ground black pepper

The Coating:
Sesame and/or nigella seeds

1. **Prepare the filling:** Mix all the ingredients. Season with nutmeg and black pepper. Salt is usually not needed because the cheeses are salty.
2. Preheat the oven to 180°C (350°F).
3. **Prepare the chukor:** Brush one sheet of the phyllo dough with olive oil. Place another sheet on top of the first one and brush with olive oil.
4. Cut the pastry sheets into two equal rectangles. Put 2-3 spoonfuls of the filling along the bottom third of each rectangle. Roll into a loose log and then shape into a spiral. Repeat with the remaining phyllo sheets to make a total of 12 bourekas.
5. Arrange the bourekas on a tray lined with baking paper and brush with the remaining olive oil. Garnish with sesame and nigella seeds and bake for about 40 minutes until golden-brown and crisp. Serve warm.

Malabi

Malabi, a creamy pudding that hails from Turkey, has established itself as Israel's most popular street dessert. Snow-white, fluttering and exotically aromatic, malabi is usually sold from specialty stalls in disposable goblets, with thick sweet syrup and various crunchy toppings. In recent years high-class restaurants adopted it and began serving richer and more sophisticated versions. Malabi is light and refreshing — the perfect finale to a summer meal.

Almost Sahlab Sahlab means orchid in both Hebrew and Arabic. Authentic hot sahlab pudding is based on a powder milled from the tubers of orchids cooked with milk and spices. Warm malabi is similar in taste and may be served as a substitute for sahlab. Follow the recipe for malabi but do not cool — serve immediately. Sprinkle some coconut flakes, cinnamon and chopped nuts on top to complete this comforting winter dessert.

Malabi

Ingredients (for 12 servings in half-cup goblets)

4 cups (1 liter, 1 quart) milk
75 g (3 oz, 3/4 cup) corn starch
1 tablespoon rose water or 2-3 drops rose essence
1 cup (240 ml, 81/2 fl oz) whipping cream

100 g (31/2 oz, 1/2 cup) sugar
To Serve:
Raspberry syrup with rose water to taste
Coarsely chopped roasted pistachio nuts
Coconut flakes

1. In a bowl, mix one cup of milk with the corn starch and rose water until the corn starch dissolves completely.
2. Bring the remaining milk together with the whipping cream and sugar to a simmer. Pour in the dissolved corn starch mix and cook 2-3 minutes over low heat, stirring constantly, until the mixture thickens.
3. Remove from the stove and pour into serving dishes. Cover with cling wrap, allow to cool to room temperature and refrigerate for at least 4 hours.
4. Serve with raspberry syrup perfumed with rose water and garnish with chopped pistachio nuts and/or coconut flakes.

Creative Malabi Basic malabi is neutral in taste, so let your imagination run free and create enticing desserts using various toppings and garnishes: berries, sliced or diced fresh fruit, fruit preserves, pomegranate seeds, candied citrus peels, etc.
Festive Malabi Prepare the malabi as described and pour into a large round-bottomed bowl. Cool and refrigerate. To serve, pry loose and turn over into a large, transparent bowl. Garnish with syrup or any of the above toppings. Or, use small shot glasses and serve two or three "shots" per diner, each one with a different garnish.

Nobody knows its real name, and everybody calls it by the name of the cross street, Dr. Erlich. For over 40 years this tiny kiosk has been the number one destination for malabi devotées. The secret recipe was brought by the owner's grandfather from Turkey.

Olive Oil
The Soul of the Mediterranean

Olives and olive oil have always been revered in Jewish culture as a symbol of beauty, fertility and peace. The olive was first cultivated in the Levant and Crete almost simultaneously. The earliest development is thought to have been in Syria by a Semitic tribe nearly 6000 years ago. From its roots in the areas of Syria, Israel and Lebanon, olive cultivation spread to Turkey, Arabia, North Africa and Spain. The Hebrew word for olive is *zayit*, which is the obvious root of the Arabic *zeit*, Armenian *dzita*, and Spanish and Portuguese *azeite*.

Olive trees grew wild in the forests of ancient Israel, particularly on the hills of Galilee, Samaria and Judea, but also in the Sharon Plain and the Negev Desert. Olive oil was used for food, cooking, medicine, illumination, hygiene and cosmetics, and for anointing kings and priests. It was also an important commodity for trade and export. There is evidence that olive oil from Canaan was exported to Egypt and Greece over 4000 years ago.

It is in Israel that the earliest mortars for crushing olives and the oldest surviving vestiges of olive wood were discovered. The oldest olive oil jars, dating back to 6000 BCE, were found in Jericho. The Philistine capital Ekron (in the central coastal plain of Israel) was the most complete olive oil production center — 114 large olive oil presses were excavated, indicating the size of the industry in ancient times. ▷

The olives are harvested by shaking the trees and beating the branches.

A good olive oil was thought to be one you could buy in a plastic bottle, usually by the side of the road. The source of the oil, or whether it was indeed olive oil, was unknown. But, if it was green enough and the smell was really strong, it was considered "the real thing".

◁ In the Israel of today place names evoke the importance of the olive: Beit Zayit — House of Olives, Har Hazeytim — The Mount of Olives, and Garden of Gethsemane (*gat shemen* — oil press) are the most famous. The emblem of the modern State of Israel depicts a menorah, an ancient oil lamp candelabra, flanked by olive branches.

Given this wealth of heritage and tradition, it is astonishing that less than twenty years ago olive oil was hardly used by the Jewish population, in stark contrast to the Israeli Arabs whose high consumption reflected their dependence on olive oil for their livelihood. The average Jewish household used small amounts of oil to season a salad. Cooking, frying or baking with olive oil was rare. In those days a good olive oil was thought to be one you could buy in a plastic bottle, usually by the side of the road. The source of the oil, or whether it was indeed olive oil, was unknown. But, if it was green enough and the smell was really strong, it was considered "the real thing". Terms like 'extra virgin' or 'cold press', let alone 'varietal olive oil', were virtually unknown.

The change came about in the last decades of the 20th Century, and it was nothing short of dramatic. During the same years that Israelis were learning to appreciate good wine and fell in love with handmade cheeses, they discovered the magic of high quality olive oil. Ironically, the catalyst was an external one. The Mediterranean diet, with olive oil its star ingredient, took global cuisine by storm and eventually arrived in Israel. Local chefs started looking for oils to suit their needs, first imported and then homegrown. Amateur cooks quickly followed suit. Quality-driven producers rose to the challenge and supplied a variety of products to the newly sophisticated market, which was willing to pay a premium for a bottle of extra virgin olive oil. Suddenly there were olive oil tastings, olive oil-based recipe contests and olive oil festivals.

Local cuisine of the third millennium is unthinkable without olive oil, as befits an eastern Mediterranean country. A fresh fish is likely to be grilled with only fresh herbs and olive oil. Chefs will use olive oil to enhance carpaccio or simply drizzle it on gourmet bread products. A small dish of olive oil may appear on the table in place of butter. Israelis will add olive oil, lemon juice and parsley to salads, unlike their European ▷

Varieties of Olives

The Souri, sometimes referred to as the Suri or Syrian olive, is the main indigenous variety, especially popular in the Galilee. It is one of the oldest varieties in the world — thought to have originated in the Lebanese town of Sur (Tyre). This small oval olive produces an aromatic piquante oil that is green and peppery with a hint of honey.

The Barnea olive was developed in Israel by Professor Shimon Lavie and went on to become an international variety planted in Australia and Argentina. Small and oblong, it is easy to grow and provides good yields. It makes a sweeter delicate oil with a fruity taste and an aroma of mown hay.

Nabali (Balladi) originated in Nablus. The improved Balladi, known as Mohsan, was introduced to Israel by the Arabs of Judea and Samaria after 1967. A larger olive than the Souri, it is easier to cultivate and milder in taste than the Souri and Barnea.

International varieties are also grown in Israel, including Manzanilla and Picual from Spain, Novo and Leccino from Italy, Fishulin from France, and Kalamata from Greece.

Ein Kammonim, Galilee

Tradition and advanced technology coexist in harmony in this beautiful Galilee farm, which is also famous for its goat cheese (see page 220). The modern mechanized oil production plant includes a 200-year-old olive press.

Ironically, the catalyst was an external one. The Mediterranean diet, with olive oil the star ingredient, took global cuisine by storm and eventually arrived in Israel.

◁ counterparts who will dress salads with oil and vinegar. There are olive oil-based bread products and even desserts, cakes and cookies. Contemporary kosher cuisine has enthusiastically adopted olive oil as a flavorful cooking and frying agent to take the place of margarine and other non-dairy substitutes for butter.

Whereas in the southern Mediterranean the custom is to use olives in cooking, in the eastern Mediterranean they are served as a starter or as part of a meze.

Today olive groves cover more than 200,000 acres, from the mountains of the Galilee in northern Israel to the Negev Desert, and from the coast in the west to the hills and valleys of the east. The largest concentration of olive groves is still in the Galilee. The most famous quality olive-growing regions are the Western and Lower Galilee, but the valleys surrounding Mount Carmel, the Sharon Plain, the Golan Heights and the Judean foothills are all now sites for the production of good olive oil. The Israeli genius for agriculture and technology come together in the Negev highlands in the initiative to plant olive groves irrigated by saline, brackish water drawn from deep wells. The resulting olive oil has won worldwide recognition for its quality.

The average harvest for the production of olive oil in Israel is about 6,000 tons, but current consumption is more than double that amount, necessitating imports. Strict quality controls are maintained by the Israel Olive Board and only products that pass their stringent tests get the 'Quality Approved Israeli Olive Oil' stamp. The Board organizes annual blind tasting competitions for both large and small producers to promote quality.

Each of the main communities — Jews, Arabs, Druse and Circassians — cultivates olives, making the industry the symbol of the melting pot that is Israel.

Connoisseurs, foodies and olive oil mavens are often surprised by the high quality of Israel's finest olive oils. They are considered to be more aromatic, more strongly flavored and full of character than the more delicate European olive oils. Once again the Eastern Mediterranean, the cradle of the olive, is producing world-class olive oil.

Land of Olives

As opposed to olive oil, which became the darling of the local cuisine only recently, olives have always been popular and widely consumed. Black olives pickled in wine or dried in salt are popular, but all-time favorites are cracked Souri olives — small, green, piquant and often homemade, they are part of every meze table and breakfast menu and a popular between-meals snack.

simple pleasures

Soups

Israel is a warm country, but we do have a winter — mild and rainy in most parts and downright cold in Jerusalem and the Galilee. For those wet gray winter days nothing beats a bowl of hot soup. Following are some of the most loved ones. One important member of the family — the ubiquitous Jewish Chicken Soup — appears in all its glory in the chapter on Shabbat (p. 193).

Harira — Moroccan Chickpea and Lamb Soup

Probably the dish that best represents Moroccan Jewish cuisine, this hearty, rich and tasty soup contains the best possible ingredients: lamb, chicken, chickpeas, lentils and rice. A complete meal — and more — in one big pot.

Ingredients (serves 12)

1/4 cup olive oil
600 g (1 lb 5 oz) lamb (shoulder or neck), cut into bite-sized chunks
3 onions, chopped
3 cloves garlic, crushed
21/2 liters (21/2 quarts) chicken stock or water
1 cup chickpeas, soaked in water overnight and drained
1 cup brown lentils
Salt and freshly ground black pepper
1 teaspoon turmeric

1/2 teaspoon dry ginger
1 teaspoon ground coriander seeds
Pinch of cinnamon
4 tomatoes, peeled and diced
12 chicken drumsticks
1/2 cup rice
To Serve:
Freshly squeezed lemon juice or 1/4 lemon per diner
Fresh chopped parsley
Harissa (p. 298) or filfel chuma (p. 296)

1. Heat the oil in a heavy pan and brown the lamb. Transfer to a large soup pot with a slotted spoon.
2. Add the remaining ingredients to the soup pot except the chicken and rice. Season and cook for one hour. The result should be a tasty, spicy soup.
3. Add the chicken and rice and cook for another 30 minutes, stirring occasionally, until the rice is soft. Taste and adjust the seasoning.
4. Before serving, add lemon juice and parsley and serve with freshly baked white bread and a hot condiment, such as harissa or filfel chuma .

Yemenite Calf Leg Soup

One of the flagship dishes of Yemenite Jewish cuisine, this soup is made from the least expensive ingredients. For maximum extraction of the bone marrow, cook the soup slowly on an electric plate or paraffin stove, preferably overnight.

Ingredients (serves 8)

2 calf's legs, cut into 4 slices each (ask the butcher)
Oil for frying
2 onions, chopped
2 teaspoons turmeric

Salt
1 teaspoon hawaij (Yemenite spice mix, p. 299)

To Serve:
Zhug (Yemenite hot sauce, p. 298)

1. Brown the calf's leg slices and onions in a large saucepan with some oil, making sure the bones do not burn. Add the turmeric and water to a height of 5 cm (2 inches) above the contents, and cook for 2 to 3 hours.
2. Taste and determine whether the marrow has been completely extracted. If desired, continue cooking over a very low heat for 8 hours or more. Add water as required.
3. Prior to serving, season with salt and hawaij and cook for another 5-10 minutes. Serve with zhug.

Bean Soup

Hot, spicy and immensely satisfying, this soup is best enjoyed with large helpings of white bread or poured over a bowl of steamed rice.

Ingredients (serves 6)

2 cups dry white beans, soaked in water overnight and drained
11/2 liters (11/2 quarts) chicken, beef or vegetable stock
2 tablespoons tomato paste
Freshly ground black pepper

1 teaspoon ground cumin
1/2 teaspoon cayenne pepper
1 teaspoon crushed garlic
Salt to taste

To Serve:
Fresh chopped parsley or coriander

1. Rinse the beans, put in a saucepan and cover with cold water. Cook for 30 minutes until partly softened, and drain. Return the beans to the saucepan, add the stock and tomato paste and season with pepper, cumin, paprika and garlic.
2. Cook for about one hour, stirring occasionally. Add stock or water if necessary.
3. When the beans have softened, mash slightly to thicken the soup. Season with salt, add the chopped parsley or coriander and serve.

Meaty Bean Soup Add 1/2 kg (about 1 lb) beef and 2-3 beef knee joint bones together with the beans.

Zecharriya and Rina, Tel Aviv

A tiny veteran eatery in the heart of *Kerem Hateymanim*, The Yemenite Quarter near the Tel Aviv Carmel Market. Famous for their traditional stews and soups cooked overnight on paraffin stoves and their airy lahukh flatbread fried on the premises.

YEMENITE CUISINE

Lentil and Vegetable Soup

A well-known Bible story tells how Esau sold his birthright to his brother Jacob for a bowl of lentil stew.

Ingredients (serves 8)

2 cups brown lentils, soaked in water for about 30 minutes and drained
2 tablespoons vegetable oil
1 leek (white part only), chopped
1 onion, chopped
2 cloves garlic, chopped
1/2 celery root, diced
1 carrot, diced
1 tablespoon tomato paste

Ground white pepper
1/4 teaspoon ground caraway
6-7 cups chicken or vegetable stock
1 thyme sprig
1 bay leaf
Salt
To Serve:
Chopped chives

1. Heat the oil in a saucepan and sauté the leek, onion, garlic, celery and carrot until golden. Add the tomato paste and fry for 4 minutes.
2. Add the lentils, season with pepper and caraway and pour in the stock. Add the thyme and bay leaf and cook for an hour and 15 minutes over low heat. Season with salt, taste and adjust the seasoning. Serve with chopped chives.

Creamy Jerusalem Artichoke Soup

Avi Steinitz, Avenue Convention Center, Airport City

Golden, smooth and creamy, this soup can also be served in espresso cups as an appetizer.

Ingredients (for 10 espresso cups or 4-6 soup bowls)

750 g (11/2 lb) Jerusalem artichoke, peeled and cut into 4 cm (2 inch) pieces
2 tablespoons olive oil
2 cloves garlic, peeled
1 leek (white part only), finely chopped
2 cups vegetable stock

1/2 cup whipping cream
Salt and white pepper
The Garnish (Jerusalem artichoke chips):
2 Jerusalem artichokes, peeled and shaved with a vegetable peeler
Oil for deep-frying

1. Heat oil in a heavy saucepan and sauté the chopped leeks until translucent. Add the garlic and sauté for one more minute. Add the Jerusalem artichokes, and sauté for a few minutes.
2. Add the stock and bring to a boil. Season with a little salt and pepper, cover and cook for 30 minutes over a low heat until the artichokes are very tender.
3. Purée the soup in a food processor and strain. Bring to a boil, add the cream, taste and adjust the seasoning.
4. **Prepare the garnish:** Heat the oil for deep-frying and fry the artichoke shavings until crisp. Drain excess oil on paper towel.

Jerusalem artichoke has nothing to do with Jerusalem, or with artichokes for that matter. Originally from North America, this tasty tuber is in fact a member of the sunflower family. *Girasole*, Italian for sunflower, sounds like Jerusalem, hence the mix-up. In Israel it has gained popularity over the last few decades, mainly in restaurants, usually as a soup or a purée.

Kubbe Hamousta

Yehuda Melamed, Kubbiya, Jerusalem

Kubbe, also known as *kibbe* or *kubba*, stands for a whole family of dumplings from Lebanon, Syria and Iraq that are served throughout the Middle East. Especially popular locally are the torpedo-shaped *kubbe halabi* with a crisp bulgur wheat shell and ground lamb and pine nut filling, and the soft semolina kubbe cooked in a soup. The latter is one of the hallmarks of Jerusalem cuisine and is served everywhere, from market eateries to fancy restaurants. The following version of traditional Kurdish Kubbe Hamousta, cooked and served in a lemony broth, comes from a trendy restaurant cum jazz club in downtown Jerusalem. The meticulous preparation of the kubbe dumplings is adapted from the book "Eating in Jerusalem" by Rina Valero.

Ingredients (serves 10-15)
The Kubbe:
1 cup coarse bulgur wheat
1 cup fine bulgur wheat
1 cup semolina
Salt
1-2 tablespoons flour
Oil for frying
800 g (13/4 lb) beef, ground finely
4-5 celery stalks (light inner ones), chopped very finely
3-4 cloves garlic, crushed

Freshly ground black pepper
The Soup:
3 tablespoons oil
5 large onions, diced
2 liters (2 quarts) clear chicken soup or water
2/3 cup freshly squeezed lemon juice
1 bunch celery stalks, sliced
1 bunch Swiss chard, cut into strips
Salt and black pepper

1. **Prepare the dough:** Mix the two kinds of bulgur and add water to 4 cm (11/2 inches) above the bulgur. Let sit for 45 minutes while the wheat absorbs the water. It should remain covered by water at all times; add more if necessary.
2. Squeeze the bulgur and discard the water. Add salt and semolina and mix thoroughly. Add the flour and knead by hand to form soft malleable dough.
3. **Prepare the filling:** Heat the oil in a large skillet and fry the meat slowly on a low heat until completely dry, about one hour. Add the chopped celery and garlic and fry for 4-5 minutes.
4. **Prepare the dumplings:** Dip your hands into cold water. Put a piece of dough the size of a small egg in the palm of your left hand and press your right thumb into its center, turning it to form a hole for the filling. Put a tablespoon of the filling in the hole and cover with the dough. Reshape into a ball and flatten slightly. Make sure your hands are wet at all times or the dough will break. Repeat the process with the rest of the dough.
5. **Prepare the soup:** Heat oil in a large pot and fry the onions until golden. Add water or stock and bring to a boil. Add the celery and Swiss chard. Season with salt and pepper. Add lemon juice gradually (the soup should be quite sour), reduce the heat and cook for about half an hour. Add the dumplings and cook for 20 minutes. Let the soup stand for at least an hour, reheat and serve (allow 3 dumplings per serving).

Another popular soup to serve with kubbe: Fry 5 coarsely sliced onions, add 6 peeled and diced tomatoes and cook slowly until the tomatoes turn to a paste. Add 2 liters (2 quarts) water and bring to a boil. Add 6 sliced courgettes and about 1/2 kg (1 lb) diced pumpkin, season with salt and pepper, and cook until the vegetables are tender (serves 6).

Couscous

Everybody loves couscous, from children who top it up with ketchup to sophisticated diners who prefer the elaborate meat and vegetable versions. Steamed couscous is used in salads, in main courses, and even in some desserts. Known in other parts of the Middle East as maftoul, it was brought to Israel by Jews from North Africa — Morocco, Libya, Algeria and Tunisia. These communities have been feuding for years over who makes the most delicious couscous dishes. Preparing couscous the traditional way is a labor-intensive, time-consuming process. Fortunately, instant couscous is readily available. The instructions are simple and the final result closely resembles the real thing. Be advised that products sold as Israeli Couscous are, in fact, toasted pasta (ptitim) and not couscous (read more on p. 126).

Making the Best of Instant Couscous

Flavoring Instead of soaking the couscous in water and oil as instructed by the manufacturer, use homemade chicken soup or vegetable stock. Oil prevents lumps, so don't omit it from the list of ingredients.

Size Instant couscous is available in three sizes: coarse, medium and fine. The fine grain is the closest to the real thing. The coarse grain is good for salads. The medium grain is suitable for all purposes.

Fluffing The stage at which you use a fork to fluff the couscous is extremely important. According to the traditional method, the grain is passed several times through a sieve. Applying this method to the instant couscous produces excellent results. Pay attention to the texture when preparing couscous for salads, where individual grains are especially important.

Serving Heap the couscous in a deep dish and arrange the solid elements of the stew (meat, vegetables) on top. Ladle the soup/sauce around the couscous but don't soak it with too much liquid or the couscous will turn into a muddy porridge.

Lea Gueta, of **Gueta**, a Tunisian restaurant in Jaffa, prepares couscous from scratch. Semolina grains are mixed with water, rubbed between the palms and passed several times through a sieve to form fine crumbs. The couscous is then mixed with oil and cooked over an aromatic broth in a special pot called a couscoussiere.

Traditional Couscous Soup

This is the vegetarian version of the exotically fragrant Moroccan soup that is served with couscous. Use the same procedure to prepare couscous soup with chicken (see below).

Ingredients (serves 6-8)

The Soup:
1 cup chickpeas, soaked in cold water overnight, rinsed and drained
4 carrots, cut into 2-3 large chunks
4 medium potatoes, quartered
1 large onion, quartered
Salt and freshly ground white or black pepper to taste
Small pinch of saffron or 11/2 teaspoons turmeric

200 g (7 oz) pumpkin , cut into 4-5 large chunks
4 courgettes, cut into 3-4 large chunks
Half a green cabbage, quartered
4-5 stalks celery stalks, peeled and cut coarsely (save the leaves)
To Serve:
1/2 kg (1 lb 2 oz) instant couscous

1. Put the chickpeas in a large saucepan, cover with water and cook for about 30 minutes. Drain, pour in 2 liters (2 quarts) of water (to prevent the soup from becoming cloudy later on), and cook for another 30 minutes, until the chickpeas are tender.
2. Add the carrots, potatoes and onion, season with salt, pepper, saffron or turmeric and cook for 45 minute s until the vegetables are tender.
3. Add the remaining vegetables (except the celery leaves) and cook for 15 minutes, until tender. Taste and adjust the seasoning. Add the celery leaves and cook for another 15 minutes.
4. Prepare the couscous according to the manufacturer's instructions.
5. Place a heap of couscous in a deep dish. Arrange the vegetables on top and ladle the soup around and over the couscous.

Red Couscous Soup When adding the pumpkin, cabbage and courgettes, add one small can (300 g, 101/2 oz) of tomatoes in tomato paste and continue according to the recipe.
Spicy Couscous Soup Add 1-2 tablespoons of filfel chuma (p. 296) or harissa (p. 298) towards the end of the cooking cycle.
Couscous Soup With Chicken Add 6-8 chicken drumsticks for the last 30 minutes of the cooking cycle.

Couscous and Roasted Vegetables Salad

Couscous is a great base for hearty and healthy salads. This one doesn't keep well and should be served immediately.

Ingredients (serves 6)

500 g (1 lb 2 oz) instant couscous, medium or coarse grain
1 eggplant, cut into 2-3 cm (1 inch) cubes
2 zucchinis, sliced
2 sweet peppers (one red, one yellow), seeded and cut into large chunks
10 whole cloves garlic, unpeeled

3 cloves garlic, crushed
1/2 cup olive oil
Salt and freshly ground black pepper
3 tablespoons pine nuts
1 red onion, sliced
1 small bunch basil leaves, cut into strips

1. Preheat the oven to 200°C (400°F).
2. Prepare the instant couscous according to the manufacturer's instructions.
3. Arrange the eggplant, zucchinis, peppers and unpeeled garlic cloves in a baking dish lined with baking paper.
4. Mix the olive oil with salt, pepper and crushed garlic and pour over the vegetables. Toss lightly to mix the sauce with the vegetables.
5. Roast the vegetables in the oven for 20 minutes or until golden. Cool slightly.
6. Roast the pine nuts in a hot frying pan, without oil, until they are golden-brown.
7. Mix the couscous with the roasted vegetables. Add the pine nuts, onions and basil and toss everything together. Sprinkle more olive oil and serve immediately.

Rice Dishes

From a simple steamed white rice that absorbs the rich sauce of a meat stew, to festive rice casseroles that are a meal in themselves, rice is found in innumerable variations in every household. Following are four simple and delicious recipes that make great side dishes. For best results use a heavy pot with a tight fitting lid. Old school cooks insist on covering the pot with a kitchen towel before closing it to ensure that no vapor escapes. If you adopt this method be careful the towel doesn't catch fire.

Mejadra — Rice with Lentils

Mejadra is usually served as a side dish, but can be a highly nutritious main course for vegetarians, or for all of us for that matter.

Ingredients (serves 6-8)

1 cup brown lentils
2 cups rice
Olive oil for frying
3 onions, chopped
1 tablespoon ground cumin

Salt and freshly ground black pepper
To Serve (optional):
2 onions, sliced into thin rings
Oil for frying

1. Cook the lentils in water until they soften, about 30 minutes. Drain and set aside.
2. Heat the olive oil in a saucepan and fry the onions until golden. Add the lentils and season with cumin, salt and pepper. Add the rice and stir-fry for a minute or two until the rice grains turn opaque.
3. Add 3 cups boiling water, bring to a boil, lower the heat, cover and cook for 20 minutes. Turn off the heat, fluff with a fork, cover and let rest for 10 minutes before serving.
4. Before serving, fry the onion rings in oil until brown and crisp and arrange over the mejadra.

Quick Mejadra If you have cooked rice on hand, use it to prepare mejadra. Cook lentils until they soften. Fry the onions, add the lentils and season. Add the rice and heat together for about 5 minutes.

Green Rice

A quick, aromatic and tasty rice dish favored by Persian Jews. What makes the rice green and fragrant is an abundance of fresh herbs, another hallmark of this unique cuisine.

Ingredients (serves 8)

3 cups rice
1/4 cup oil
1 large onion, chopped finely
3 cups fresh herbs (parsley, dill and coriander), chopped finely

1 teaspoon salt
1/2 teaspoon ground cumin
1/2 teaspoon freshly ground black pepper
1/2 teaspoon turmeric (optional)
3-4 cardamom pods, crushed

1. In a heavy saucepan, heat the oil and sauté the onion until light golden. Add the herbs, spices and 41/2 cups of boiling water.
2. Cook for about 10 minutes, taste and adjust the seasoning. The broth should be salty and spicy.
3. Add the rice and cook over medium heat until it has absorbed the liquid. Stir the rice with a fork to distribute the herbs evenly.
4. Cover and cook for 10 minutes on minimum heat. Turn off the heat, fluff the rice with a fork, cover and let rest for 10 minutes.

Green Rice with Meat or Chicken Sauté the onions and add 700 g (11/2 lb) diced shoulder of beef, pre-cooked until tender, or a whole chicken divided into 8 parts. Brown the meat or the chicken and continue according to the recipe above.

Red Rice

This is the dish children love best, even after they are grown and have children of their own. Cook the rice in homemade chicken soup for best results.

Ingredients (serves 6)

2 cups rice
1/3 cup oil
1 large onion, chopped
3 tablespoons tomato paste

3 cups chicken or vegetable stock
1 teaspoon paprika
1/2 teaspoon ground cumin
Salt and freshly ground black pepper

1. Heat the oil in a saucepan and fry the onions until golden brown. Add the tomato paste and fry for 3-4 minutes, stirring frequently.
2. Meanwhile, bring the chicken stock to a boil.
3. Add the rice to the saucepan with the fried onions and tomato paste. Mix, season, and add the boiling stock. Cover, lower the flame and cook for 15 minutes. Fluff with a fork, cover and let rest for 10 minutes before serving.

Rice with Crispy Noodles

This is a wonderful way to cook and serve rice. The rice is white and soft, the noodles golden-brown and crispy. The best part is what sticks to the bottom of the pan.

Ingredients (serves 6)

2 cups rice
31/4 cups chicken or vegetable stock
50 g (2 oz) margarine or butter
1/4 cup oil

1/2 cup thin noodles (angel hair or vermicelli)
Salt

1. Bring the chicken stock to a boil.
2. Heat the oil and butter (or margarine) in a saucepan, add the noodles and fry until brown and crispy. Add the rice and continue frying only until the rice is hot. Season with salt, add the boiling stock, cover the pan and cook for 20 minutes over low heat.
3. Place a flame tamer (simmer ring) under the pan, spread a kitchen towel under the lid and cook for another 20 minutes. Fluff with a fork, cover and let rest for 10 minutes before serving.

Ptitim — The Israeli Couscous

Pearls, loops, stars and even hearts, Israeli toasted pasta comes in many shapes, but the original ptitim (literally little bits or flakes) were shaped like grains of rice. Indeed, in the fifties when this unique Israeli invention first came on the local market, it was dubbed "Ben-Gurion Rice" after the first prime minister of Israel. The story goes that Ben-Gurion came up with the idea to manufacture a substitute for rice, which was in very short supply during that time of rationing. A different version of the story, probably closer to the truth, is that the nickname was given by new immigrants who were not happy to eat ptitim instead of the real thing.

Over the years ptitim have maintained their image as a homey, not to say kiddy, side dish, the hit of the kindergarten lunch menu, preferably with a generous dollop of ketchup. It therefore came as a shock to many Israelis when this humble staple made its way to the trendiest restaurants in New York and London, where it was reborn as "Israeli Couscous". Touted as the "in-grain for the new millennium" (even though it is not a grain), it is served with posh ingredients and sold in gourmet food stores.

Ptitim are versatile and easy to work with. The texture is pleasant and the baking lends them a nice nutty flavor. They can be boiled like pasta in a large amount of water, or prepared pilaf-style by first frying them, usually with onions, and then cooking them in boiling water or stock until all the liquid is absorbed. Their neutral flavor makes them a perfect partner for almost any ingredient and condiment.

Ptitim with Mung Beans

This recipe is similar to Italian Risi e Bisi (rice and peas risotto). Ptitim replace the rice and mung beans take the place of the garden peas.

Ingredients (serves 4-6)

1 cup mung beans
4 tablespoons oil
2 large onions, chopped
3 cloves garlic, chopped
1 cup fresh herbs (parsley, coriander, dill, mint and sage), chopped finely
5 cups vegetable or chicken stock
500 g (1 lb 2 oz) ptitim, preferably rice shaped
Salt and crushed black pepper

1. Bring mung means to a boil in a large amount of water. Drain and set aside.
2. Heat the oil in a saucepan, add the onions and sauté until they become translucent.
3. Add the garlic and herbs and sauté for another 2 minutes.
4. Add the ptitim and continue frying for 3 more minutes. Add the mung beans, stir lightly, add the stock and bring to a boil. Continue cooking on a very low heat for about 25 minutes until all the liquid is absorbed and the ptitim are tender. Turn off the heat, wait a few minutes and serve.

Ptitim Casserole with Chicken and Vegetables

Like regular pasta, ptitim have a neutral flavor and it takes spices and herbs to bring them to life. This recipe makes a complete dinner in a single pot, all done in 30 minutes.

Ingredients (serves 4-6)

4 tablespoons oil
2 large onions, chopped
2 carrots, chopped
1 cup fresh mushrooms, sliced
1 chicken breast, cut into small dice
2 tomatoes, grated
2 cups ptitim

1 teaspoon hawaij (Yemenite seasoning mix p. 299)
1/2 teaspoon curry powder
1/2 teaspoon turmeric
Salt and freshly ground black pepper
21/4 cups boiling chicken stock or water
1/4 cup fresh coriander, chopped

1. Heat the oil in a saucepan, add the onions and sauté lightly. Add the garlic, carrots and mushrooms and sauté for another 4 minutes until golden. Add the chicken and stir-fry until it turns white.
2. Add the tomatoes, ptitim and spices, stir and pour in the boiling stock or water. Mix, taste and adjust the seasoning. Bring to a boil, lower the heat, cover and cook for about 20 minutes, until the liquid is absorbed and the ptitim are tender.
3. Fluff with a fork, add the chopped coriander, cover, and wait another 10 minutes before serving.

Fish

Jewish cuisine holds fish in high regard, and some of the best dishes of Jewish communities are built around fish. Harsh conditions in the fledgling State of Israel seem to have changed all that. In the early days of austerity and rationing, fresh fish, with the exception of pond-grown carp, were virtually nonexistent. The market offered mainly frozen slabs of unnamed imported fish fillets, and a whole generation of Israelis grew up believing that "fillet" was a kind of tasteless fish. For many years fish was far less popular than poultry or beef in Israeli homes and restaurants. Specialty fish restaurants, usually located by the sea and run by colorful seafaring owner-chefs, did spring up here and there but they were few and far between.

As time went by, fish, and especially saltwater fish containing iodine, omega-3 fatty acids and other beneficial nutrients, came to be regarded as healthy. This, together with increasing exposure to international cuisines, made fish popular once again and the demand for fish rose dramatically. As quality fresh fish have become readily available, owing largely to the rapid advances in fish farming (see more on p. 138), chefs and amateur cooks use fish much more frequently — and enthusiastically — than ever before.

In true Mediterranean fashion, Israelis in a restaurant prefer whole, fresh fish, grilled or fried on the premises. They will squeeze lemon juice on top and usually forgo any other sauce. Upscale restaurants offer elaborate and creative fish and seafood dishes, including the latest favorite — raw fish.

Fisherman's Wharf
in Akko

Chreime – North African Hot Fish Stew

Chreime made from grouper, amberjack or some other fine fish is featured at Rosh Hashanah and Passover dinners in the households of North African Jews (from Morocco, Libya, Algeria, Tunisia), but the sauce is so delicious and dominant that inexpensive fish may be used. Indeed, everyday versions of chreime prepared with cheaper kinds of fish can be found in market eateries and workers kitchens, and of course at home. Bear in mind that the fish should be juicy when ready, so the cooking time must be adapted to the type of fish: the leaner the fish, the shorter the cooking cycle.

The dominant spices in chreime are paprika, cayenne pepper and garlic, but the secret ingredient that never fails to give the sauce the touch of authenticity is ground caraway. Don't omit it!

Ingredients (serves 4-6)

1 kg (2 lb 4 oz) fish with white, firm flesh (grouper, greater amberjack, sea bass, grey mullet or even carp), cut through the bone into thick slices (steaks)
1/3 cup oil
10 cloves garlic, crushed

2 tablespoons paprika
1 tablespoon (or less) cayenne pepper
1 teaspoon ground caraway
1 teaspoon ground cumin (optional)
2-3 tablespoons tomato paste

1. Heat the oil in a large wide saucepan, add the garlic and spices and fry over high heat while stirring until the oil becomes aromatic. Add the tomato paste and stir until the paste blends with the oil. Add one cup of water and cook covered for 5 minutes.
2. Carefully add the fish steaks to the sauce, bring to a boil, cover and lower the heat. If the sauce does not completely cover the fish steaks, turn them once halfway through the cooking.
3. Cook for 10 minutes or until the fish is done but still firm and juicy. Serve with couscous or steamed rice and a lot of soft white bread for mopping up the sauce.

Uri Buri, Old Acre

Buri is grey mullet. Uri (Jeremias) is the name of
the owner-chef. Uri Buri is one of the best-loved
fish restaurants in the country. Uri buys the fish at
the picturesque Acre market, or straight from the
fishermen's boats.

Trout Casserole

Uri Jeremias, Uri Buri, Acre

Before gilthead sea bream became the darling of local chefs, trout from the crystal-clear waters of the Dan River in northern Israel was the fish of choice. This recipe has nothing particularly Israeli about it except that it is one of the signature dishes at Uri Buri. Besides, it's extremely easy to make and so good.

Ingredients (serves 2)

4 pink trout fillets, with skin
1 tablespoon butter
The Sauce:
12/3 cups whipping cream
1 teaspoon coarsely ground peppercorns
(white, red, black and green)

1 flat teaspoon anchovy fillets, crushed
1 teaspoon Nam Pla fish sauce (optional)
To Serve:
Spring onion, chopped finely
Chives, chopped finely

1. Heat a heavy saucepan over medium heat and when very hot, spread the butter on the bottom.
2. Place the trout fillets in the saucepan, skin side down, put the lid on and turn the flame up. After one minute, shake the saucepan, continue cooking for 2-3 minutes and remove from the stove. Remove the lid.
3. Mix the cream with spices and anchovies in a bowl or a saucepan and warm in a microwave oven or on the stove until slightly thick.
4. Put two trout fillets on each plate, pour some of the sauce over them, garnish with chopped spring onion or chopped chives and serve.

Serving Suggestion Add boiled rice to the bowl of sauce. Mix well and serve with the fish.

Tip Instead of chopping the anchovy fillets, put them in a garlic press. The bones will stay in the press and the chopping board and knife will remain clean.

Gilthead Sea Bream Baked with Pickled Lemon Sauce

Dror Piltz, Food Writer

Known locally as *denis*, gilthead sea bream has become synonymous with fresh saltwater fish in Israel, being widely cultivated on fish farms and sold everywhere. The following recipe can be prepared with a variety of saltwater fish, but it's the sauce based on lemons preserved in salt that makes it special. This extremely tasty and versatile specialty from Moroccan cuisine can be bought at Middle Eastern grocery stores, at supermarkets in Israel, or you can make your own (p. 296).

Ingredients (serves 4)

4 whole gilthead sea breams or other portion-size firm-fleshed saltwater fish, gutted and cleaned thoroughly
Coarse sea salt
Freshly ground black pepper

8 tablespoons pickled lemon spread (p. 296)
12 cloves garlic (or more)
1 lemon, sliced very thinly
8 rosemary sprigs

1. Preheat the oven to 220°C (425°F).
2. Cut 4 sheets of aluminum foil, each large enough to wrap a whole fish. Place one fish on each sheet, season with salt and pepper and spread on a generous amount of the pickled lemon spread.
3. Fill the cavity with cloves of garlic, lemon slices and sprigs of rosemary. Wrap the fish with the foil, folding the edges to seal the fish.
4. Bake for 15 minutes, open the foil and bake for another 5 minutes, until the skin is crisp and golden-brown. Serve immediately.

Fish Ceviche with Eggplant Cream

Avi Biton, Adora, Tel Aviv

Ceviche, a South American raw fish delicacy, took international cuisine by storm, and Israel was no exception. The following is a very local take on this dish. The tangy taste of the marinated fish combined with the velvety, slightly smoked eggplant cream is pure delight.

Ingredients (serves 3-4)

The Fish Ceviche:
200 g fillet of fresh firm-fleshed saltwater fish (greater amberjack, meagre), cut into 1 cm (1/2 inch) cubes
1 tomato, peeled, seeds removed, diced
1 small red onion, chopped finely
Juice of 1 lemon
6 tablespoons olive oil
Pinch of crushed dry chili pepper
Salt
1/2 cup fresh coriander, chopped

The Eggplant Cream:
1 eggplant
4 tablespoons olive oil
1/4 cup whipping cream
1 tablespoon freshly squeezed lemon juice
Salt

1. Mix the ingredients for the ceviche, excluding the coriander.
2. Roast the eggplant over an open flame (see instructions on p. 31). When the flesh is tender, scoop it out and blend it with the olive oil, whipping cream, lemon juice and salt in a food processor.
3. Pour the eggplant cream into the center of a plate, put the ceviche on top, garnish with the chopped coriander and serve.

Variation Add 1/2 cup cooked lentils to the ceviche.

Fishing in Israel

From the Mediterranean to the Sea of Galilee, from the Hula swamp and the rivers flowing down from the Golan Heights to the Red Sea, fishing has been a major source of food for the region since the dawn of history. Hebrew Scriptures refer to fishing activity in the country's coastal cities in the Roman-Byzantine period. Bones of fish in two Roman forts in the Judaean Desert, Matsad Tamar and Ein Bokek, attest to the transport of fish from the Mediterranean and the Red Sea.

Fishing in modern Israel is another story. While Arab fishermen continue to keep the ancient tradition alive, the drastic decline in the fish population of the Eastern Mediterranean has fostered a thriving economy of aquaculture — intensive cultivation of fish under controlled conditions, mainly in ponds. Actually, keeping and growing fish in artificial ponds and pools has been practiced in the region since ancient times. Visits to such places as Caesarea, Nahliel Island at Rosh Hanikra, Akhziv and Dor turn up the archeological remains of pools hewed out of the rocky Mediterranean coastline. Freshwater ponds were built inland for freshwater fish. These ponds were used for keeping fish, rarely for rearing them from fry, although there is evidence that techniques of fish rearing were known in ancient times.

Intensive fish growing in ponds was first attempted in modern Israel in 1939 at Kibbutz Nir-David in the Jezreel Valley. Since those humble beginnings, Israel has become a world leader in intensive fish farming. For many years the main species grown in freshwater ponds was the common carp. With time, additional fish species were introduced to the market, mainly from intensive growing in ponds and massive stocking of the Sea of Galilee: silver carp, grass carp, grey mullet, St. Peter's fish, rock bass, silver perch and Barramundi. The last two are recent arrivals from Australia.

Another fish farming method involves the growing of fish in special cages submerged and anchored in the sea. Such facilities have been in operation since the late 1970s in both the Mediterranean and the Red Sea. Species grown by this method include the popular gilthead sea bream (locally known as *denis*), European sea bass, and a South American variety of meagre.

The most exotic method of growing fish commercially in Israel involves special ponds with porcelain-tiled walls that utilize the running water of the Dan, a tributary of the Jordan River. The water is routed through canal-like ponds, creating a naturally oxygenated habitat suitable for species that normally inhabit fast-flowing rivers, like trout and salmon.

As commercial fishing in the eastern Mediterranean is sadly becoming a thing of the past, the supply of fresh fish to the Israeli market now depends almost entirely on aquaculture. Thanks to on-going research and developing technologies, Israeli fish farming is meeting the growing demand for quality table fish.

Fishing in the Sea of Galilee

Chicken

It's safe to say that the vast majority of meat consumed in Israel is chicken, with turkey a close second. Even today frozen poultry is sudsidized and its prices are government controlled — a carry-over from the days when it was the only affordable source of animal protein. Times have changed, beef and lamb are readily available, but chicken still reigns supreme. Every family has a collection of recipes for every occasion — from quick lunch dishes to elaborate casseroles.

Roasted Chicken Drumsticks in Carob Syrup

Carob trees grow everywhere in Israel, and their fruit, naturally sweet and rich in fibers and vitamins, is used to make a number of food products (even a chocolate substitute). Carob syrup, delicately sweet, dark and very thick, is a wonderful addition to salad dressings, marinades and desserts. Try to find it in health-food stores. If unavailable, use a combination of honey, soy sauce and orange juice (see below).

Ingredients (serves 4-6)

12 chicken drumsticks
6 cloves garlic, halved
The Marinade:
3/4 cup carob syrup
1/4-1/3 cup chicken stock

1 teaspoon coriander seeds, crushed coarsely
3 cloves garlic, crushed
2 sprigs rosemary, chopped coarsely
Salt and freshly ground black pepper

1. Make 2-3 incisions on each drumstick and insert half a clove of garlic into each.
2. Mix the marinade ingredients, pour over the chicken and let it marinate in the refrigerator for a minimum of 6 hours.
3. Preheat the oven to 200°C (400°F).
4. Arrange the drumsticks on a rack and roast for 30-40 minutes until golden-brown and juices run clear when the meat is pricked with a fork.

Variation Substitute the carob syrup with 1/2 cup honey, 1/4 cup freshly squeezed orange juice and 2-3 tablespoons soy sauce.

Chicken Casserole with Dried Fruit on a Bed of Couscous

Inspired by Moroccan Tajin cooking, this dish contains modern additions: wine, balsamic vinegar and soy sauce. Like the Moroccan original, it is served over a bed of couscous, which lovingly absorbs the rich sauce. Chicken is considered "everyday" food, but this dish is fit for the most festive occasion.

Ingredients (serves 4-6)

12 chicken drumsticks
6 whole, small red onions, peeled
12 pieces (each 4-5 cm/2 inches long) of Jerusalem artichoke, peeled
250 g (9 oz) dried figs
200 g (7 oz) prunes
200 g (7 oz) dried apricots

The Marinade:
1/2 cup oil
2 tablespoons sesame oil
2 tablespoons brown sugar
3 tablespoons honey
1/2 cup soy sauce

5 cloves garlic, chopped
3 sticks cinnamon
1 tablespoon coriander seeds
1 level teaspoon turmeric
1 tablespoon cumin seeds, crushed
2 tablespoons sesame seeds
Salt and freshly ground black pepper
1/4 cup balsamic vinegar
2 cups dry red wine

To Serve:
1/2 kg (1 lb 2 oz) instant couscous
1/2 cup walnuts, roasted

1. Mix all the ingredients for the marinade.
2. Arrange the chicken, onions, Jerusalem artichoke and dried fruit in a baking dish and pour over the marinade. Cover and refrigerate for a minimum of 3 hours, up to 24 hours.
3. Preheat the oven to 180°C (350°F).
4. Bake uncovered for 40 minutes or until the chicken turns shiny and brown. Baste the chicken occasionally with the liquid from the bottom of the pan. The dish up to this point may be prepared in advance and later heated in the oven.
5. Before serving, prepare instant couscous as per the manufacturer's instructions.
6. Arrange the chicken casserole and sauce over a mound of couscous, sprinkle the walnuts on top and serve immediately.

Chicken with Olives

A Mediterranean classic. Go easy on the salt as the olives are salty.

Ingredients (serves 6)

6-8 chicken parts
1/2 cup olive oil
2 cloves garlic, finely chopped
4 tomatoes, peeled and diced
2 tablespoons tomato paste

450 g (1 lb) green olives, washed
thoroughly and pitted
Salt and finely crushed black pepper
2 cups chicken stock
1/2 cup fresh parsley, chopped

1. Heat 1/4 cup olive oil in a wide saucepan. Add the garlic, sauté for one minute and add the tomatoes. Cook for about 3 minutes, add the tomato paste and bring to a boil, stirring constantly.
2. Arrange the chicken parts in the saucepan. Add the olives and pour in the remaining oil. Season, taking care not to use too much salt. Pour in the chicken soup, making sure the contents of the pan are covered with liquid, and cook for 30 minutes or until the sauce thickens. Add the parsley and cook for another 5 minutes.
3. Serve over a mound of couscous or steamed rice.

Chicken Albondigas in Tomato Sauce

Small, soft, melt-in-your-mouth chicken dumplings from Jerusalem Sephardic cuisine. In this version they are cooked in a piquant tomato sauce.

Ingredients (serves 4)

The Chicken Dumplings:
300 g (101/2 oz) ground chicken (breast or deboned thighs)
1 potato, finely grated and squeezed
1 onion, grated
2 cloves garlic, chopped
1 egg
6 tablespoons breadcrumbs
1 teaspoon turmeric
Salt, white pepper and coarsely ground black pepper

The Sauce:
3 tablespoons oil
1 onion, chopped finely
3 cloves garlic, chopped
3 tablespoons tomato paste
2 cups crushed tomatoes
3 tablespoons soy sauce
2 tablespoons paprika
1 level teaspoon ground cumin
2 tablespoons sugar
Salt and coarsely ground black pepper

1. **Prepare the chicken dumplings:** Mix all the ingredients, knead thoroughly and roll into balls the size of walnuts. Refrigerate for 30 minutes.
2. **Prepare the sauce:** Sauté the onion until translucent. Add the garlic, tomato paste, crushed tomatoes, soy sauce, spices, sugar and 1 cup water and bring to a boil.
3. Add the dumplings to the sauce and cook covered over a low heat for 30 minutes. Gently shake the pan from time to time but do not stir. Serve with white rice, mashed potatoes or lots of bread.

Stuffed Vegetables

In Hebrew they are called *memulaim*, meaning "stuffed ones", the word synonymous with the simple delicious fare at which our grandmothers excelled. Originally devised to stretch cheap, readily available ingredients into a meal for the whole family, stuffed vegetables are venerable members of traditional Jewish cuisine — from the Balkans to Morocco, from East European stuffed cabbage leaves to Syrian stuffed eggplants in pomegranate sauce. They can be time-consuming to prepare but the results never fail to impress and delight. Chefs love them too. And no wonder, as they invite innumerable variations of color, taste and texture.

Balkan-style Stuffed Peppers

Being naturally hollow, peppers are perfect candidates for stuffing. Simple ingredients, minimal seasoning and straightforward preparation come together here to produce this Balkan favorite.

Ingredients (serves 4-5)

8-10 sweet peppers (preferably the light green, thinner skin variety)

The Stuffing:
1 onion, chopped
1/4 cup oil
1 cup rice
250 g (9 oz) beef, ground finely
1 tomato, grated
3 tablespoons fresh parsley, chopped

1 teaspoon paprika
Salt and freshly ground black pepper
1 teaspoon baharat spice mix (p. 299)

The Sauce:
3 tablespoons (1 small tin) tomato paste
2 cloves garlic, crushed
Pinch of sugar
Salt and freshly ground black pepper

1. Cut the wide bases off the peppers to form lids and set aside. Remove the white membrane and seeds and discard.
2. **Prepare the stuffing:** Fry the onions in oil until golden, add the rice and stir until it becomes opaque. Add the ground meat and fry for about 5 minutes, crumbling the meat with a fork. Add the grated tomato, chopped parsley and spices. Mix well and remove from the stove.
3. **Prepare the sauce:** Put the tomato paste, garlic and spices in a wide shallow saucepan, add 1 cup water and bring to a boil.
4. Stuff each pepper to three-quarters its capacity (the rice swells during cooking) and arrange the peppers close together in the saucepan containing the sauce. Spoon some of the sauce over the stuffing and cover each pepper with its lid.
5. Bring to a boil, cover the saucepan and reduce the heat. Cook for about one hour, until the rice is done (but not mushy). Occasionally spoon some of the sauce over the stuffing to prevent it from drying out.

Stuffed Baby Eggplants and Courgettes in Pomegranate Sauce
Benny Saida, Cookbook Author

A delightful combination of eggplants and courgettes stuffed with meat and rice and cooked slowly in a tangy pomegranate sauce. This recipe is by one of the most prolific and respected cookbook authors in Israel, and he learned it as a child in Tiberias, from his grandmother Esther.

Ingredients (serves 10)

15 courgettes
10 baby eggplants
Oil for frying
2 onions, sliced thinly
2 tomatoes, sliced

The Stuffing:
11/2 cups long grain rice
300 g (101/2 oz) beef, ground finely
3 tablespoons oil

1/2 cup fresh parsley, chopped
Salt and freshly ground black pepper
1/2 teaspoon turmeric

The Sauce:
Freshly squeezed pomegranate juice or
1/2 cup pomegranate concentrate diluted
in water, enough to cover the contents
1/3-1/2 cup freshly squeezed lemon juice
Salt and freshly ground black pepper

1. Cut off the stalks of the courgettes and scoop out the flesh using a corer.
2. Cut off the stalks of the eggplants, but leave the green leaves untouched — they will keep the eggplant from falling apart while the flesh is being removed. Scoop out the flesh using a melon baller or a tablespoon, and only then take off the green leaves.
3. Mix the ingredients for the stuffing. Stuff the vegetables to three-quarters their capacity and fry until golden.
4. Line a wide, flat saucepan with the onion and tomato slices. Arrange the stuffed vegetables on top and pour 1/4 cup oil into the pan. Season with salt and pepper, cover the contents with the freshly squeezed pomegranate juice (or the diluted pomegranate concentrate), and add the lemon juice.
5. Bring to a boil and cook covered over the lowest heat for about 5 hours, until the contents are dark brown and there is a small amount of thick sauce remaining on the bottom of the saucepan.

Vegetables stuffed with ptitim
(recipe on p. 154)

Vegetables Stuffed with Ptitim (Israeli Couscous)
Daniel Zach, Carmella Bistro, Tel Aviv

A colorful casserole of vegetables stuffed with *ptitim* (Israeli couscous, see p. 126), cooked in a rich sauce. In his restaurant Daniel stuffs the vegetables with organic spelt pasta flakes; in addition to being extremely healthy, they retain their shape even after long slow cooking. Ordinary ptitim work just as well. Another healthy and delicious option is wheat (recipe below).

Ingredients (serves 6-8)
6 small beetroots
6 sweet peppers (red, yellow and green)
6 turnips
6 large Jerusalem artichokes
The Stuffing:
1 large onion, chopped
2 cloves garlic, crushed
250 g (9 oz) ground lamb
250 g (9 oz) ptitim (Israeli couscous)
3/4 cup fresh parsley, chopped
5 tablespoons olive oil
1/2 teaspoon baharat spice mix (p. 299)
1/2 teaspoon turmeric
1/2 teaspoon salt

The Cooking Sauce:
1 onion, sliced
3 cloves garlic, crushed
2 tomatoes, grated
5 tablespoons olive oil
1 tablespoon sugar
1 tablespoon tomato paste
2 teaspoons paprika
1 teaspoon cayenne pepper
1/2 teaspoon ground cumin
1/2 teaspoon turmeric
Salt
3 liters (3 quarts) chicken or lamb stock

1. **Prepare the stuffing:** Sauté the onions in olive oil until they turn translucent. Add the garlic and spices, mix well and allow to cool.
2. Add the rest of the ingredients and mix well.
3. **Prepare the vegetables for stuffing:** Cut the wide bases off the peppers to form lids and set aside. Remove the white membrane and seeds and discard. Peel the Jerusalem artichokes. Peel the turnips and beets, leaving the stalks attached. Cut off the tops to form lids and set aside. Using a melon baller, scoop out the flesh of the turnips, beets and artichokes.
4. Stuff the vegetables to three-quarters their capacity and arrange close together with their lids in a large wide pan. Tie any leftover stuffing in a cheesecloth and place in the pan; it will absorb the sauce and make a great side dish.
5. **Prepare the sauce:** Sauté the onion in the oil until golden. Add garlic and spices and mix well. Pour in the stock, bring to a boil and simmer for 5 minutes. Taste and add salt.
6. Pour the sauce over the vegetables to three-quarters their height. Bring to a boil, cover tightly, turn the heat down very low and cook for an hour and a half until the vegetables are tender but retain their shape.

Wheat Stuffing Replace the ptitim with an equal amount of wheat, soaked overnight in cold water, drained and rinsed.
Serving Suggestion For an elegant occasion, serve the stuffed vegetables alongside grilled lamb chops (see photo opposite).

Figs Stuffed with Bulgur and Cranberry Salad

Figs, fresh or dried, with their sweet luscious flesh and firm skin, are perfect for stuffing. Here is a light healthy dish to start off a summer meal.

Ingredients (serves 10)

10 fresh figs
Pomegranate concentrate, for serving
The Salad:
100 g (31/2 oz) bulgur wheat
1/2 cup dried cranberries, chopped coarsely

1 cup carrots, grated coarsely
2-3 tablespoons fresh coriander, chopped
1 tablespoon sesame seeds, roasted
3 tablespoons pecans, chopped
2 tablespoons pomegranate concentrate

1. Soak the bulgur wheat in water for 4-5 hours, until it swells up and softens. Or, add half a cup of water to the wheat and cook in a microwave oven for 3-4 minutes until the bulgur softens and absorbs the water. Allow to cool.
2. Mix the bulgur with the other salad ingredients. The preparation up to this point may be done in advance and the salad kept in the refrigerator.
3. Halve the figs and scoop out some of the flesh, which you can add to the salad. Place two fig halves on each plate, heap on the salad, sprinkle with pomegranate concentrate and serve.

Bread
From Standard to Sourdough

Lechem Achid, "standard bread," is the name for the basic loaf of bread: still subsidized by the government, still sold at some neighborhood bakeries by the half-loaf, still missed by Israelis abroad. It may be mass produced today but its distinctive taste and texture still retain some of the original charm, especially when oven fresh.

In the olden days home baking was the norm in Palestine. People would buy flour in bulk or take their own wheat to a nearby mill to be ground into flour for a bread they baked at home in a brick or mud oven. Small commercial bakeries did exist in the *yishuv*, the Old Settlement in Palestine. One of the earliest was Berman's of Jerusalem, established around 1875, that evolved from a cottage industry of home-baked bread and cakes for Christian pilgrims.

As the *yishuv* developed and urbanized with the arrival of waves of immigrants in the 1920s and '30s — mainly from Eastern and Central Europe — every new neighborhood had its own bakery. Expert Jewish bakers from Poland and Germany labored to produce handmade sourdough bread for the population, making delicious loaves accessible to all even in a time of economic hardship and general frugality.

Modern industrial ovens on an assembly line replaced the old brick ovens in the newborn State of Israel, and mass-produced bread replaced the handmade sourdough loaves of the veteran bakers. The process of industrialization, similar to what was happening in the rest of the Western world, continued for decades, making bread readily available but robbing it of its traditional taste.

In the 1980s, as travel became more common, people began implementing some of what they learned abroad. Small boutique vineyards, fine restaurants, and specialist dairies and bakeries sprang up, offering fare the likes of which the ▷

Erez Komarovsky — one of the leading figures in the local bread revolution.

◁ country had never seen or tasted before. Leading the quality bread trend was Tushiya Bakery of Tel Aviv, offering German-style breads to discerning individuals. Soon the irresistible fragrance of freshly baked bread was wafting out of small up-scale bakeries all over the country. Handmade bread was back — with a vengeance!

The leading figure in the gourmet bread revolution was Erez Komarovsky, founder of Lechem Erez (Erez Bread). This fine bakery in the European tradition offered rich handmade sourdough breads, often embellished with olives, cheese, fresh herbs or sun-dried tomatoes. Lechem Erez went nationwide in no time at all. The success of his old-world methods and products infused energy into existing boutique bakeries and encouraged the opening of new ones, even in the most unlikely locations. Some up-market cafés — another dramatic culinary trend — now offer a wide range of fresh breads and pastries baked on the premises.

Various ethnic groups continue to produce traditional breads. Lavash, the chunky flatbread of the Jews from the former Soviet Republic of Georgia, is a notable example. Other communities from the former USSR, Ethiopia and India also have special regional breads. The Arabs have their own specialties — mostly flatbreads, but crusty loaves as well.

So, in just one century, Israeli bread evolved from a simple basic necessity to a highly refined delicacy. The variety is simply mind-boggling and the quality high. For the time being small specialist bakeries are managing to survive competion with industrial giants. Whether this coexistence will last only time will tell. Meanwhile, everyone can enjoy a practically infinite selection of fine breads.

Bar Lechem, Tel Aviv

Friday rush at one of the latest additions to the boutique bread scene. A selection of delectable sourdough breads, rye bread, breads with nuts, olives and raisins, brioche and even low-calorie bread that still tastes like the real thing.

grill

The Israeli *Mangal*

Itzik Hagadol (The Big Itzik), Tel Aviv
A typical meal in this popular steak house in downtown Tel Aviv starts with a battery of meze salads, followed by a selection of skewered grilled meats.

Long before steak houses (*steakiyot*) became popular in the early 1960s, Arab restaurants throughout Israel grilled shishlik and kebab as well as fish. But grilled meat was not their exclusive domain. In Kerem Hateymanim, the Yemenite Quarter in central Tel Aviv, small eateries like Tzarum specialized in meat grilled and served on metal skewers. There were similar places in every neighborhood where Jewish immigrants from Middle Eastern countries lived. Using wood for fuel, they set up simple grills on the sidewalk to attract customers with the aroma of cooking meat while those dining inside were spared the smoke.

Later on, barbecue stands began cropping up along main roads. Nothing more than an improvised grill, a table and a tub of ice and soft drinks, they offered Israelis what became one of their favorite pick-ups: grilled meat stuffed in a pita. Many of these stands established themselves as full-fledged restaurants in gas stations and kept going for decades.

At the same time, Israel's first luxury hotels introduced a new concept to a country indoctrinated in a Spartan lifestyle: five-star grillrooms. These high-class establishments quickly became the meeting places for the "cream" of society: politicians, industrialists, bankers, lawyers and generals rubbed shoulders with shady characters with spare cash.

This cosmopolitan import quickly spread beyond hotels and sirloin steaks and hamburgers became available throughout the land. For the first time, Israelis realized that grilled meat does not have to be charred, and "rare" and "medium" soon became part of everybody's vocabulary. ▷

What Israelis love most is to make their own barbecues. Locally called *mangal or al ha'esh* (over the fire), they have become the country's leading participant sport.

A barbecue stall in the Old City of Jerusalem

◁ In the 1970s, Shkhunat Hatikva, a modest neighborhood in south Tel Aviv, gained fame for its unique barbecue scene. Dozens of kosher restaurants along Etzel Street, the area's main drag, offered more or less the same menu: fresh Iraqi pita from the bakery down the road, an extensive assortment of salads and dips, and a selection of meats grilled on metal skewers ranging from chicken livers, hearts and spleens, turkey testicles and cows' udders, to a unique local invention, grilled foie gras. For many Israelis the idea of an evening out was a good, reasonably priced meal at one of these restaurants. This dining style is still popular in Shkhunat Hatikva and throughout the country.

Over the years imported tastes brought a variety of newcomers to the field: Argentinean-style Asado grill restaurants, Brazilian-style all-you-can-eat grills, and dozens of American-style eateries specializing in steaks and giant hamburgers. They joined veteran Balkan and Middle Eastern restaurants serving a variety of grilled meats, including different versions of a local favorite, lamb kebabs.

The huge demand for meat suitable for grilling gave rise to some unique inventions, one involving a product known locally as *pargiyot*, literally meaning "spring chickens". Many people still believe these are a different breed of poultry, or chickens slaughtered while they are young. In reality, they are the meat cut off the thighs of ordinary chickens; the name was thought up by restaurateurs to add chic to mundane poultry. This dark meat with a relatively high fat content is much better for grilling than lean chicken breasts.

Restaurants and grillrooms aside, what Israelis love most is to make their own barbecues. Locally called *mangal* or *al ha'esh* (over the fire), they have become the country's leading participant sport, taking place in the backyard, on the balcony, on the beach or on a picnic. Wherever you go, on any given weekend or holiday (weather permitting), you will see sweaty men hunched over cheap, box-like barbecues, frantically fanning the coals to cook massive quantities of grilled meat for large groups of family and friends. This phenomenon reaches its peak on Independence Day, when the barbecue crowds occupy every bit of grass and shade, deploying their grills, chairs and tables, intent on getting down to business.

Regardless of class, style, taste or cost, barbecue remains one of Israel's best-loved food categories. It can safely be said that grilled meat has evolved into a mainstay not just of Israeli cuisine, but of Israeli lifestyle.

Grilled Chicken Wings

Chicken wings are perfect for barbecuing and therefore popular the world over. The following recipes use typical Middle Eastern ingredients.

Ingredients (for 25 wings, 4-6 servings)

Chicken Wings in Za'atar
1/2 cup olive oil
3 tablespoons za'atar (hyssop spice mix, p.299)
Salt and freshly ground black pepper

Chicken Wings in Sumac
1/2 cup olive oil
3 tablespoons sumac
Salt and freshly ground black pepper

Chicken Wings in Baharat
2 tablespoons ground allspice
1/2 teaspoon ground nutmeg
1/2 teaspoon ground cardamom
1/2 teaspoon cinnamon
Pinch of ground cloves
1/2 cup olive oil
Salt and freshly ground black pepper

Barbecue Flavored Chicken Wings
1/2 cup sunflower or corn oil
2 tablespoons paprika
11/2 teaspoons cayenne pepper
1 teaspoon ground cumin
5 cloves garlic, crushed
Salt and freshly ground black pepper

Mix all the ingredients and soak the wings in the marinade for at least 4 hours. Skewer (to make turning on the grill easier) and grill over a hot charcoal grill or under the broiler in an oven set to 220°C (425°F).

Marinades for Pargiyot (deboned chicken thighs)

Israelis prefer chicken to beef for grilling, and rightly so. Chicken meat is more forgiving when cooked on a simple charcoal grill, and skewered chicken thighs (*pargiyot*) cut in chunks are by far the best. Most barbecue aficionados season during the grilling by sprinkling spiced oil over the meat or rubbing it in with half an onion. It is advisable to marinade the meat in advance, for at least an hour and up to 24 hours. Here are two ideas.

Olive Oil, Garlic and Herb Marinade

1/2 cup olive oil
3 cloves garlic, minced
The crumbled leaves from 5 sprigs of thyme
Salt and crushed black pepper

Pickled Lemon and Paprika Marinade

1/2 cup pickled lemon spread (p. 296)
1 tablespoon sweet paprika
1/4 cup oil

Mix all the ingredients and soak the meat in the marinade for 2-4 hours. Skewer and grill over a hot charcoal grill or under the broiler in an oven set to 220°C (425°F). You may alternate chicken chunks with fresh vegetables such as cherry tomatoes, red onions, zucchini and sweet peppers.

Grilled Stuffed Cornish Hens

Shay Assael, Mevashlim Havaya Cooking School

When grilling large chunks of meat or whole chickens, make sure there is enough distance between the source of heat and the rack, or the chicken will burn on the outside before getting done inside.

Ingredients (serves 5)

5 Cornish hens
300 g (101/2 oz) chicken livers, cubed
1 tablespoon oil
Cloves from 2 heads of garlic, peeled
2 onions, each cut into 6 wedges
1 cup fresh parsley, chopped
6 tablespoons pistachio nuts, roasted

Salt and freshly ground black pepper
The Coating:
1/4 cup olive oil
1 tablespoon ras-el-hanoot (Moroccan spice mix, p. 256)
4 tablespoons soy sauce
2 tablespoons honey

1. Sauté the livers in hot oil. Cool and mix them with the garlic, onions, parsley, nuts and spices.
2. Stuff the chicken with the mixture and secure with a toothpick.
3. Mix the coating ingredients and brush the skin. Refrigerate for 30 minutes.
4. Barbecue slowly over an elevated grill rack for 2 hours, turning once or twice. The chicken is ready when the juices run clear when pricked with a fork.

Nashat Abbas from El Baboor (left) and Dokhol Safadi from Diana

It's only half an hour drive between **Diana** in Nazareth and **El Baboor** in Um-el-Fahem, two of the best Arab restaurants in Israel. Both attract diners from all over the country, both preserve age-old traditions of Palestinian cooking, both are proud to use unique local ingredients such as wild edible plants, and both are best avoided on weekends when they are packed with patrons. Both serve unique delectable kebabs that have become synonymous with their establishments.

Diana Lamb Kebab

Dokhol Safadi, Diana, Nazareth

Diners grow weak with hunger just watching the butcher/grillman. He stands right in the middle of the restaurant, deftly dissecting fresh lamb portions, chopping them with a huge cleaver, adding spices, shaping the kebabs and threading them onto long metal skewers. The grilled kebabs are removed from the skewers with a laffa and served immediately, juicy and irresistible.

Ingredients (serves 4-6)

1 kg (2 lb 4 oz) fresh lamb (shoulder or thigh, with the fat), chopped with a knife or ground coarsely
2 large onions, chopped coarsely
2/3 cup fresh parsley, chopped finely

1 cup pine nuts, roasted
1 teaspoon black pepper, crushed
1/2 teaspoon baharat spice mix (p. 299)
1 heaping teaspoon salt

1. Mix all the ingredients and knead for 4-5 minutes. Shape into long or round kebabs and thread onto metal skewers.
2. Barbecue on a charcoal grill about 3-4 minutes on each side. Serve with grilled onions and tomatoes and tahini dip (p. 38).

El Baboor Lamb Kebab

Hussam and Nashat Abbas, El Baboor, Um-El-Fahem

The inspiration for this dish is Syrian *kebab halabi,* grilled and then baked in a spicy tomato sauce. Hussam and Nashat introduced a few delicious changes: grilled tomatoes and onions for the sauce and a disk of pita dough to seal the baking dish. In the following home version, use pita or laffa bread to seal the dish and wrap it tightly with aluminum foil.

Ingredients (serves 4-6)

1 kg (2 lb 4 oz) fresh lamb (shoulder or thigh, with the fat), chopped with a knife or ground coarsely
3 cloves garlic, minced
1 hot green pepper, chopped finely

1 teaspoon salt
1/2 tablespoon baharat spice mix (p. 299)
4-5 large ripe tomatoes
2 onions, quartered
1-2 large Iraqi (laffas) or regular pitas

1. Mix the meat with half the hot pepper and garlic, season with baharat and salt and shape into oval kebabs.
2. Roast the tomatoes over an open flame or on a charcoal grill. Peel and chop coarsely. Season with the rest of the garlic and hot pepper.
3. Preheat the oven to 200°C (400°F).
4. Skewer the kebabs, alternating them with onion quarters. Grill 3-4 minutes on each side until the kebabs are half-done.
5. Remove the kebabs and onions from the skewers and transfer to a deep baking dish or ovenproof earthenware plate together with the roasted tomatoes. Cover the dish with a pita, wrap with aluminum foil and bake for 10 minutes. Serve immediately.

Variation: To prepare the dish as it is served in the restaurant, follow the recipe for pita dough (p. 84) but do not bake it. Roll out the dough to a disk large enough to seal the top and sides of the baking dish. Sprinkle with sesame and/or nigella seeds and bake as instructed.

Fruits of Paradise

Everyone knows that eating the fruit of the Tree of Knowledge brought about the expulsion of Adam and Eve from the Garden of Eden. But what exactly was that fateful fruit? Western tradition says it was the apple. Other theories mention a fig — luscious and sexy, it would definitely fill the bill, as would a pomegranate, which looks like a treasure box laden with precious stones, or a date with its sleek skin and honey-sweet flesh.

All these contenders for the "fruit of paradise" and many more flourish in Israel. Some are relative newcomers, others have been around since the dawn of civilization. Carbonized remains of figs almost 11,500 years old were recently excavated by archeologists near the town or Jericho, making them the oldest known domesticated crop.

Israel is a tiny country but a long and narrow one with a variety of topographies and climates. The fruit bounty is accordingly diverse. Apples, cherries, plums, nectarines and other deciduous fruit trees as well as berries (a recent addition) prevail in the cool mountainous Galilee and Golan Heights. Move 20-30 miles south and you reach Lake Kinneret (The Sea of Galilee) and the Jordan Valley where date palms reign supreme in the subtropical heat, with banana plantations a close second. Avocados and mangos also abound there as well as along the northern Mediterranean coastline. Farther to the south in the lower Galilee, with its softly rolling hills and relatively dry climate, olive and almond groves dot the Biblical landscape. The finest almonds in Israel are called Um-El-Fahem, and it is said that the best almond trees are ▷

Fruit picking season in northern Israel: dates and mangos from the Jordan Valley, apples and nectarines from the Golan Heights

The finest almonds in Israel are called "Um-El-Fahem", and it is said that the best almond trees are all children of one famous giant that still grows in the town of Um-El-Fahem in the Ara Valley.

◁ all children of one famous giant that still grows in the town of Um-El-Fahem in the Ara Valley. Almond trees also abound in the Jerusalem mountains, their rose-white blossoms heralding the coming of Spring.

The coastal plain and the Sharon region once looked like one huge citrus grove dotted with a few scattered settlements. Today, as the cost of land in central Israel sky-rockets, many of these groves are giving way to real estate ventures. But there are still plenty of *pardesim* (Hebrew for citrus groves), which in Spring fill the air with the intoxicating smell of orange blossoms, and in Winter look equally seductive, heavy with golden fruit, leaves shiny from the rain.

Our journey continues south to the Lakhish Valley, home of plump juicy Lakhish table grapes, and on to the desert, once completely fruitless but today the site of cutting-edge agricultural research projects. The sweetest, most luscious cherry tomatoes are grown here, irrigated by water drawn from deep artesian wells. Apparently the salinity of the brackish water is responsible for the exceptional sweetness of the fruit. Most of these tomatoes are exported to Europe where they fetch a hefty price.

And let's not to forget the figs and the pomegranates, venerable members of the "Seven Species" club (along with dates, grapes, olives, wheat and barley). Both grow wild and domesticated all over the country. Pomegranates are currently enjoying a renaissance as the world discovers their healing properties and learns to enjoy their tangy charm. Another fruit in vogue is the persimmon. Israel is one of the biggest exporters of this ultra-sweet meaty fruit. Persimmon (*afarsemon* in Hebrew) is mentioned in Hebrew Scriptures in connection with perfumery in the ancient town of Jericho. But scientists tend to believe that the modern persimmon bears no connection to its ancient namesake.

Last but not least is the prickly pear, which grows wild all across Israel. Its Hebrew name, *tzabbar*, became the nickname for native Israelis who, like the fruit, are prickly and rough on the outside, sweet and tender inside.

Israelis love their fruit. The average Israeli consumes 158 kilograms (over 300 pounds) of fruit every year. And thanks to the variety of climates and geography and the know-how spurred by economic necessity, they can enjoy an infinite variety of fresh fruits year round, at prices among the lowest in the Western world. More than 40 kinds of fruit are grown on a total of some 200,000 acres, mainly in the northern part of the country, giving an annual yield of 500,000 tons (excluding citrus).

Since the beginning of the Zionist Enterprise, orchards and plantations have been a leading sector of agriculture in the Land of Israel. Visions of fruit orchards and profitable plantations in an arid land sometimes dictated the course of history for the fledgling settlement. Mulberry trees were planted in Palestine for the first time in the late 19th Century when Baron Rothschild's advisors thought silk spinning mills could be a viable industry. The silk industry never took off, but old mulberry trees can still be found in many backyards. The Baron provided a livelihood for the settlers he brought from Europe to the area of Zichron Yacov by developing vineyards; the area still abounds in grape growing and wine production. Attempts to grow exotic tropical fruits like papaya, guava, lychee, feijoa, mango and anona date as far back as the 1930s. Many other European, tropical and subtropical fruits such as pineapple, blackberry, raspberry and cherry have been grown in Israel for many years.

Israel today is a heavily industrialized, densely populated country, relying on export of sophisticated technology rather than avocados and oranges. Stiff competition in international markets combined with high labor and production costs create a harsh reality for the growers. Many choose to uproot the trees or sell the land. Others, more enterprising or more tenacious, invest in new varieties, seeking out niche markets for premium fruits, or combine agriculture with tourism. But the importance of agriculture always went beyond economics: the ideology was and is that only by working and sustaining the land does one earn the right to call it home. ▷

The Land of Oranges

Almost every fruit growing in Israel has an interesting story, intimately woven into the fabric of local history, but none is as intriguing as that of the citrus fruit, one of the symbols of modern Israel.

The first reference to citrus fruit in ancient Jewish texts dates to the Hasmonean period (166-63 BCE) and describes the citron (*ethrog*), grown in the vicinity of Jaffa and used for ritual purposes. The Arab conquerors in the 7th Century imported the first orange trees to the area, and by the late 18th Century oranges grown around Jaffa were already famous for their quality. The emergence of the Shamouti orange in the 19th Century (probably as a result of grafting with the local Balladi varieties) and the opening of the Suez Canal made Palestine a major exporter of oranges to the world. The Shamouti orange, shipped to Europe via Port Said, was an overwhelming success.

In 1855, Sir Moses Montefiore, a famous Jewish philanthropist from England, purchased the first Jewish-owned orange grove near Mikve-Israel Agricultural School. The representatives of the Baron Rothschild also encouraged planting orange groves in the new settlements. On the eve of World War I there were almost 7500 acres of orange groves, of which about one-third was the property of Jewish settlers. The citrus industry had become the main source of revenue for the Jewish community in Palestine.

The ensuing years told a tale of successes and failures. The setback caused by World War I, when not a single crate of oranges was exported, was followed by a renewed surge of planting with the addition of grapefruits, lemons and tangerines. Between the two world wars, citrus accounted for 75% of all exports from Palestine and new processing plants provided more than 110,000 jobs (the entire Jewish population of Palestine at that time was about 500,000).

The industry again fell into decline during World War II when all trade connections between Palestine and its export markets were severed. By the end of the war irrigation systems had deteriorated, crop yields were low and quality was a far cry from its former glory. Substantial investments rebuilt the industry and by 1947-48 citrus export was reinstated to its prewar level, only to be brutally interrupted again by the outbreak of Israel's War of Independence in May 1948.

By 1949, the citrus groves throughout the country were badly neglected and yields were practically nil. On the bright side, the citrus industry was the only sector capable of offering jobs to tens of thousands of demobilized soldiers and new immigrants. New groves began to be planted at the rate of thousands of acres a year and by the early 1970s, citrus covered more than 100,000 acres. About a million tons were exported under the familiar brand name "Jaffa", which became synonymous with high quality citrus fruit. Citrus growing was again Israel's leading export industry.

This success was sadly short lived: in the 1980s, fierce competition, increasing shipping distances and restrictive trade agreements brought the industry into decline once again. Many growers abandoned their groves to seek sources of revenue.

During the late 1980s and 1990s, "easy peelers" became popular in fresh produce markets. In addition to old favorites like Temple and Minneola, Israeli agricultural R&D developed several new fruit varieties. The market loved these new contenders. Today after many years of decline, there is a renewed spirit of optimism in the citrus industry, partly due to new and innovative sources of irrigation for the groves. In 2006 about 2000 acres of new citrus groves were planted, hopefully heralding a better time for this ultimate symbol of Israeli agriculture.

shabbat

Israeli Shabbat

Like any other Jewish holiday, Shabbat (Sabbath) starts at sundown the previous day. But the weekend mood sets in even earlier, on Friday morning, as everyone gears up for the commanded day of rest. In observant households Friday is a race against the clock to finish shopping, cooking and cleaning before sunset when all work must cease. Others can afford to take it easy. Friday can be a leisurely brunch with friends, reading the weekend papers in a café, or a shopping spree in a local market or mall followed by a long siesta. Typical Saturday pastimes may include an outing to the beach or a picnic in a pastoral setting, visiting relatives and friends, or attending a football match.

And yet there is one institution sacred to the majority of Israelis, religious or otherwise: Friday night dinner. Families gather, usually at the home of parents or grandparents, and attendance is mandatory! Some families have alternative traditions like Saturday brunch or lunch, or on sunny days a cookout. Whatever the timing and the circumstances, the concept is the same: a good home-cooked meal providing a chance for everybody to meet, catch up on the latest news, and give a big hug to the kids. Older "kids" already living on their own often leave with neatly packed leftovers that will last them for days.

Every family has its Shabbat favorites, many of which can be found in other chapters of this book. Here the emphasis is on classic Shabbat dishes: challah bread, chicken soup, chopped liver, hamin casseroles, and a selection of cakes. Cake-baking, another great local tradition, is especially evident on the weekends.

Challah

This soft sweet-smelling bread is the ultimate symbol of Shabbat. Some buy it on Friday mornings along with the weekend newspapers, some go to the trouble of baking it from scratch. Even kindergarten children knead and braid miniature challahs for the *Kabbalat Shabbat* (welcoming the Shabbat) ceremony. Braided challah is associated with Shabbat, while a round one, symbolizing the cycle of seasons and wishes for a good and successful year, is reserved for Rosh Hashanah (Jewish New Year). Baking challah at home requires some effort, so if you're already going to the trouble, bake a rich sweet challah that's as good as any cake.

Sweet Challah

Hans Bertele, Gaya Patisserie Shop, Petach Tikvah

Ingredients (makes 2 loaves)

1 kg (2 lb 4 oz, 7 cups) flour
40 g (12/3 oz, 31/2 tablespoons) yeast, dissolved in lukewarm water
85 g (3 oz, 1/3 cup + 1 tablespoon) sugar
2 eggs

10 g (2 teaspoons) salt
350 ml (12 fl oz, 11/2 cups) milk
85 g (3 oz) butter, softened
1 egg, beaten, for brushing
Sesame seeds or poppy seeds for garnish

1. Mix the flour with the yeast mixture, sugar, eggs, salt and milk in a mixer bowl.
2. Fit the mixer with a kneading hook and knead the dough for about 5 minutes. Add the butter and continue kneading at slow-medium speed for another 5 minutes. Cover and allow to rise for 20 minutes.
3. Knead the dough for a few minutes and allow to rise for 5 minutes. Divide into two equal balls. Cover and allow to rise for another 20 minutes.
4. Preheat the oven to 50°C (120°F).
5. **For a round challah:** Roll the dough into a thick log about 5 cm (2 inches) thick and 50 cm (20 inches) long. One end of the log should be thicker than the other. Put the thicker end in the center of an oiled, round baking dish and wrap the log around itself to form a spiral.
For a braided challah: Divide the dough into 4, 6 or 8 parts. Roll each part into a log about 25 cm (10 inches) long and braid them all into a plaited loaf.
6. Brush the loaves with the beaten egg and allow to rise for about 30 minutes in the warm oven. Brush again with beaten egg.
7. Raise the oven temperature to 200°C (400°F).
8. Brush the challah loaves again with the beaten egg, sprinkle poppy or sesame seeds on top, and bake for 35-40 minutes or until the loaves are golden-brown. The challah is ready when tapping on its bottom produces a hollow sound.

Challah With Raisins Add 1 cup raisins towards the end of the kneading cycle.

Citrus Flavored Challah Add grated peel of one orange together with the eggs. Add 1 cup of chopped candied citrus peels towards the end of the kneading.

Parmesan Challah Use only half the amount of sugar. Add 1 cup of grated Parmesan cheese towards the end of kneading, and knead one more minute.

Non-dairy (Parve) Challah Substitute water for the milk and use 45 ml (3 tablespoons) of oil instead of butter.

Lendner Bakery, Jerusalem

Situated in the ultra-orthodox Mea Shearim Quarter, this is one of the oldest bakeries in Jerusalem, with ovens dating back to the late 19th Century. This strictly kosher establishment bakes only challah bread and accordingly operates only before Shabbat — from Thursday evening to Friday noon. Yeshivah students often stop by in the middle of the night to buy a loaf just out of the oven.

Jewish Chicken Soup

Novels, plays, movies and Jewish mothers through the ages have extolled the virtues of chicken soup: pure solace on a cold winter's day, and the proven remedy for a cold, sore throat, stomachache, and even a broken heart. Here is how to produce this fragrant, golden, magical elixir.

Chicken Soup Secrets

Chicken: Chicken for soup must be fresh (smell it!), and neither too young nor too fatty. Some people use a whole chicken, but cheaper parts like wings and necks will do just fine. Frozen chicken may be used as well, but will make a less tasty soup.

Other Meats: For a meatier flavor, add turkey parts like necks and wings to the chicken. Beef cuts such as ribs or breast will give an even more pronounced meaty flavor.

Bones: Use chicken, turkey, and beef knee joint bones.

Vegetables: The more the better: onions, leeks, carrots, celery root, parsley root, pumpkin, courgettes, tomatoes and even fennel.

Herbs: Parsley, dill and celery leaves are always used. Coriander, thyme and rosemary are optional.

The Double Bouquet Trick: Divide the herbs into two bouquets. Add the first one at the beginning of the cooking cycle and remove when the cooking is done. Add the second one to the prepared soup for extra aroma.

Seasoning: Salt and peppercorns are mandatory. Allspice and bay leaves are optional. Season sparingly, especially at the outset, and adjust the seasoning towards the end of cooking after the ingredients have released their flavors.

Water: For soups in general, and for this soup in particular, use mineral, purified or filtered water to avoid aftertaste.

Cooking: Some cooks simply put all the ingredients in a large stockpot and cook everything together. Others prefer to boil the chicken first, skim the foam and only then add the vegetables. This makes skimming easier. In either case, start with the water at room temperature to ensure maximum extraction of the chicken flavors; putting chicken into boiling water locks all the flavors inside. Lining the stockpot with herbs spreads the aroma evenly. If you intend to serve the chicken parts cooked in the soup, remove them while they still retain their texture and succulence. Boiled chicken may be served with the soup or used to prepare a variety of hot and cold dishes.

Clarity: Strain the soup only after it has cooled down a bit. Vegetables in hot soup are very soft and will fall apart; they become a little firmer when cool.

Storing: Transfer the soup to the refrigerator as soon as possible to prevent souring. The solid layer of fat that forms on top can be skimmed with a spoon. You may want to keep that fat in a jar to use in other dishes.

From Soup to Stock: Always prepare plenty of chicken soup. Do what professional chefs do: strain the soup, transfer to a sealed jar or plastic container, and store in the refrigerator for up to a week or freeze. Not only does the taste get stronger after a day or two, you have an excellent basic stock on hand for future soups and sauces.

Classic Jewish Chicken Soup

The abundance of vegetables and fresh herbs, as well as a combination of chicken, turkey and beef, make this soup especially flavorful.

Ingredients (serves 8-10)

1 kg (2 lb 4 oz) fresh chicken and/or turkey parts, washed thoroughly
2 beef knee joint bones
1 bunch dill
1 bunch parsley
1 bunch celery leaves (including stalks)
1 onion quartered
2-3 carrots, cut coarsely

1 fennel bulb, cut coarsely
1 leek, cut coarsely
1 celery root, cut coarsely
1 parsley root, cut coarsely
2 bay leaves
10 black or white peppercorns
3 berries allspice
Salt

1. Line the bottom of a large pot with half the herbs (dill, parsley and celery) and place the chicken and turkey parts and beef bones over them. Add 21/2 liters (21/2 quarts) of water and bring to a boil. Skim the foam that forms on top.
2. Add the vegetables, bay leaves, white and black peppercorns and allspice, and bring again to a boil. Cook covered on a low heat for about an hour and a half. Towards the end of cooking, taste and adjust the seasoning.
3. Turn off the heat, remove the herbs from the soup and add the remaining half of the herbs. Cover and allow to stand for 15 minutes. Serve, or cool, strain and refrigerate or freeze for various uses.

Polish Chicken Soup Remove the chicken parts after one hour of cooking. Allow them to cool and tear or cut into strips. Add thin noodles (angel hair, vermicelli) to the soup and cook for 2-3 minutes. Add the chicken strips and serve.

Middle Eastern Chicken Soup Add the juice of half a lemon and one tablespoon of mint and/or coriander leaves to each bowl of soup.

Mediterranean Chicken Soup Add some grated tomato, minced garlic and 2-3 basil leaves cut into strips to each bowl of soup.

Gondi —
Chicken and Chickpea Dumplings in a Broth

One of the most delicious dishes of Iranian Jewish cuisine traditionally served on Shabbat — giant, fluffy, exotically flavored chicken and chickpea dumplings cooked and served in a fragrant yellow chicken broth.

Ingredients (serves 6-8)

The Broth:
2 chicken legs
1 cup chickpeas soaked in water overnight
2 onions, peeled
2 courgettes cut into large chunks
1 teaspoon turmeric
Salt

The Gondi:
2 onions, grated and squeezed

500 g (1 lb 2 oz) ground chicken, preferably deboned chicken thighs
1 cup dry powdered chickpeas (available in healthfood and spice shops)
1 teaspoon ground cardamom
1 teaspoon ground cumin
1 teaspoon turmeric
Salt and white pepper
1/4 cup oil

1. Place the chicken legs, courgettes and chickpeas in a large pot. Season with turmeric and salt, add 11/2 liters (11/2 quarts) water and bring to a boil. Skim the foam and cook over a low flame for about one hour.
2. Mix all the ingredients for the dumplings with 1/3 cup water. Wet your hands and form dumplings the size of an apricot (the dumplings will swell considerably during the cooking).
3. Add the dumplings to the boiling soup and bring again to a boil. Lower the heat and cook for about an hour and a half with the pot half covered.

Chopped Liver

This Ashkenazi delicacy is a classic starter for a Shabbat dinner, for Passover Seder Night and for Rosh Hashanah. It also makes a terrific snack with a cold glass of beer. For a crumbly texture use a meat grinder. For a smooth pâté use a food processor. For a lumpy texture grate or chop with a knife and then mash with a fork.

Traditional Chopped Liver

Ingredients (serves 6-8)

500 g (1 lb 2 oz) fresh clean chicken livers
4 onions, chopped coarsely
1/3-1/4 cup oil or goose fat
Salt and freshly ground black pepper
4 hard-boiled eggs

Options for Garnish:
Sliced cucumbers, grated radishes, grated hard-boiled eggs, chopped fresh onions, crunchy fried onions

1. Heat the oil or goose fat in a frying pan, add the onions and fry until golden.
2. Add the livers and fry for about 10 minutes over a low heat until they turn brown and begin to fall apart. Season with salt and pepper.
3. Using a slotted spoon, remove the livers and onions and refrigerate for a minimum of 30 minutes. Save the fat.
4. Chop livers, onions and hard-boiled eggs with a knife and mix well. Or, use a food processor, or a meat grinder fitted with a disk with medium-sized holes. Stir in some of the fat used for frying. Taste and adjust the seasoning.

Crunchy Chopped Liver Just before serving mix the chopped livers with chopped, browned crunchy *grivenes* — fried bits of goose or chicken skin and fat, also known as *grivelach.*

Chicken Liver Pâté Add 2 tablespoons brandy and purée the livers, onions and eggs until smooth. Transfer to a terrine dish lined with cling wrap and refrigerate for a few hours. Before serving, turn over onto a serving dish, remove the wrap, slice into portions and serve with toast. Berry sauce, fruit marmalade or pears poached in sweet wine complement the taste.

Chicken Liver and Nut Pâté The addition of nuts — walnuts, pecans, cashews and the like — refines the taste of the pâté and adds nice aroma. Lightly roast 1/2 cup of nuts and process with the rest of the ingredients. Reserve some whole roasted nuts for garnishing.

Hamin — Shabbat Casseroles

The Jewish religion strictly forbids the lighting of fire on Shabbat. The same rule holds for electrical sparks, so electrical appliances and mechanical devices of all kinds are also forbidden. On the other hand, Shabbat lunch is a very important meal. Traditionally, the men of the family return from morning prayers at the synagogue and the whole family gathers around the table for a weekly meal that is second in importance only to Friday night dinner.

So how do you prepare a proper meal when you are not allowed to cook or even heat up the food? Over the years, Jewish communities in places as far apart as Poland and North Africa devised and perfected Shabbat dishes that have a few things in common:

• They utilize residual heat or some other source of heat available during Shabbat, beginning the cooking Friday afternoon and ending it just before Saturday lunch.

• All the casseroles are hearty and usually quite heavy. They will make you sleepy, which is fine since there is nothing better to do on a Saturday afternoon.

• They are all based on food saved during the week to enhance the Shabbat lunch: fatty meat or poultry that requires lengthy cooking, legumes like beans and chickpeas, potatoes, bones for flavor, eggs, and grains such as wheat, pearl barley, oats and rice.

Many of us have heard the stories of how, on Friday afternoons, grandma would tote a huge cast-iron pot filled with goodies to the local kosher bakery, where she would queue up with the other housewives and wait for the baker to put the pot in the hot oven just before he turns it off for Shabbat. The hamin pots of the entire community would cook slowly overnight. The same queue would appear just after Saturday morning prayers and wait for the baker to return from synagogue and pull the pots out of the oven. Grandma would carry the steaming pot home and straight to the table, where the family would exclaim over the mouth-watering aroma and dig into the pot for choice cuts.

Other heat sources for cooking Shabbat casseroles are the old faithful single-flame paraffin stove, affectionately known by its brand name as the Primus stove; the more modern electric hot plate that gives a good steady source of heat; and an ordinary kitchen oven turned on before Shabbat and left all weekend on a very low temperature.

The most famous Jewish Shabbat casserole is the Ashkenazi cholent. Similar dishes from other parts of the world include Moroccan skheena (literally, Arabic for "hot stuff"), Tunisian bekaila, Sephardic sofrito and Iraqi thbit.

In modern Israel hamin in all its variations is still popular, not only in religious households. There is something irresistibly homey about this hearty casserole. It is definitely worth trying, especially on a grey wet weekend.

Classic Ashkenazi cholent in Tel Aviv "Mul Eden" restaurant

Cholent — Ashkenazi Hamin

There are as many versions of this casserole as there are households. All the ingredients for traditional cholent are readily available, except the *kishke* — intestines stuffed with a mixture of flour, onions, chicken, goose fat and spices. It may not sound appetizing, but this ultimate "poor man's" ingredient is one of the best parts of the cholent. Look for it in a Jewish kosher delicatessen.

Ingredients for a 6-Liter Pot (serves 8-12)

1/3 cup oil

2 large onions, chopped coarsely

1 kg (2 lb 4 oz) beef brisket or roast, cut into large chunks

350 g (12 oz) large white beans, soaked in water overnight

3-4 veal marrow bones

1 whole head garlic, halved crosswise (unpeeled)

1 teaspoon salt

11/2-2 tablespoons paprika

1 liter (1 quart) chicken or beef stock or water

8 medium potatoes, halved

300 g (10 oz) pearl barley, washed and drained

1 package stuffed *kishke*, thawed (optional)

1. Heat the oil in a large ovenproof pot and fry the onions until golden-brown. Add the meat and bones and brown on all sides.
2. Add the beans, garlic and spices. Pour in the stock or water until it covers the meat, bring to a boil and cook for one hour over low heat. Skim any fat and froth that bubbles up.
3. Add the potatoes, cook for another 15 minutes, add the pearl barley and cook for another 15 minutes, stirring occasionally.
4. Blanch or fry the stuffed *kishke* and place over the stew.
5. Preheat the oven to 100°C (225°F).
6. Cover tightly and transfer the pot to the oven for the night.

Chicken Cholent Replace the meat with 1 kg (2 lb 4 oz) of chicken parts, but do not omit the veal marrow bones.

Smoked Cholent Add 150 g (5 oz) of diced smoked goose breast, kosher cabanos sausage or some other smoked meat during the preliminary frying of the meat.

Hamin Macaron — Chicken and Noodle Hamin

This simple Sephardic hamin is visually appealing and delicious.

Ingredients (serves 4-6)

500 g (1 lb 2 oz) spaghetti or macaroni
1 chicken cut into 8 parts
Salt and freshly ground black pepper
Oil for frying
2 onions, sliced
10 whole cloves garlic, unpeeled
2 sweet or regular potatoes, cut into 2 cm

(1 inch) thick slices
4-6 hard-boiled eggs, peeled
1/2 cup chicken stock or water
1/2 teaspoon turmeric
1/2 teaspoon cinnamon

1. Cook the pasta in boiling water with salt for about 5 minutes until it begins to soften. Drain and rinse in cold water.
2. Season the chicken with salt and pepper, fry in hot oil in a large ovenproof pot until golden-brown and remove from the pot. Put the onions and garlic cloves in the same pot and fry until golden-brown. Remove from the pot.
3. Add the potato slices, season with salt and pepper and fry on both sides until golden-brown. Arrange in a single layer on the bottom of the ovenproof pot.
4. Add the pasta, return the chicken parts, onions and garlic. Add the eggs. Mix the stock with the turmeric and cinnamon and pour in. Bring to a boil.
5. Preheat the oven to 100°C (225°F).
6. Cover tightly and transfer the pot to the oven for the night. Before serving, remove the lid, place a large serving plate over the pot and turn the hamin over, in one piece, onto the plate.

A winter afternoon in the Mahane-Yehuda Market in Jerusalem

Skheena — Moroccan Hamin

The method is quite similar to Ashkenazi cholent, but the spices are typically Middle Eastern and chickpeas replace the barley.

Ingredients (serves 8-12)

1/3 cup oil
1 large onion, diced
1/2 kg (1 lb 2 oz) beef brisket or roast, cut into large chunks
4 veal marrow bones
8 potatoes, peeled
200 grams (7 oz) dry chickpeas, soaked in water overnight

1 teaspoon paprika
1 teaspoon turmeric
1/2 teaspoon ground cumin
1 teaspoon salt
1/2 teaspoon freshly ground black pepper
1-2 dry chili peppers or 1 teaspoon cayenne pepper (optional)
8 fresh eggs

1. Heat the oil in a large ovenproof pot and fry the onions until golden-brown.
2. Add the meat and bones, potatoes and chickpeas. Pour in enough water to cover the contents, season and bring to a boil. Cook for one hour over low heat.
3. Add the whole eggs and cook for another 10 minutes.
4. Preheat the oven to 100°C (225°F).
5. Cover tightly and transfer the pot to the oven for the night.

Variations
• Add 2-3 sweet potatoes together with the regular potatoes.
• Replace the meat with 3-4 chicken legs, but don't omit the veal marrow bones.

Sofrito

A rich festive dish from Jerusalem Sephardic cuisine. The cooking cycle is shorter than for hamin so it is usually served on Friday night, but it can survive in the oven overnight and be served for Saturday lunch. The technique of deep-frying the potato wedges described here is worth adopting in other dishes (for example, root vegetables in various meat casseroles). Deep-frying retains the shape and texture of the vegetables even after long slow cooking.

Ingredients (serves 8)

11/2 kg (3 lb 5 oz) beef brisket cut into large chunks
1/3 cup oil
8 small whole onions, peeled
10 whole cloves garlic, peeled
3/4 cup chicken/beef stock or water
1 teaspoon paprika

1 teaspoon turmeric
1/2 teaspoon curry powder
1/2 teaspoon ground white pepper
1/2 teaspoon ground allspice
Salt and freshly ground black pepper
8 potatoes cut into uniform wedges
Oil for deep-frying

1. Heat 4 tablespoons of oil in a frying pan and brown the beef on all sides.
2. Generously grease a wide, flat ovenproof saucepan (use 5 tablespoons of oil) and lay in the meat, onions and garlic.
3. Mix the stock or water with the spices, pour over the chicken and bring to a boil. Taste and adjust the seasoning. Cover and cook for one hour over low heat. If more liquid is needed, add some boiling water. Up to this point, the dish may be prepared in advance and kept in the refrigerator.
4. Preheat the oven to 150°C (300°F).
5. Heat the oil for deep-frying and fry the potato wedges until golden. Transfer to paper towel to drain the excess oil.
6. Arrange the deep-fried potato wedges over the cooked beef, cover the pan and transfer to the oven for about 2 hours. Or, set overnight on an electric hotplate or in a 100°C (225°F) oven. Shake the saucepan once or twice during the cooking so the sauce covers the potatoes. The sofrito is ready when all of the pieces are tender.

Chicken Sofrito Substitute the beef with 16 chicken drumsticks.

Azura, Jerusalem
This veteran market eatery serves sofrito only on Fridays, and most of it is taken out for weekend meals at home. The sofrito is still cooked the traditional way, on a paraffin stove.

A Cake for Shabbat

The enticing aroma of baking on Friday afternoons is etched into every Israeli's childhood memories. Home baking has always been a great local tradition, finding expression in the informal "Drop-by-for-coffee-and-cake" invitation. And, mind you, the cake must be homemade.

Even in the Spartan conditions of the early kibbutz, many women insisted on demonstrating their culinary skills by baking cakes and kept "cake notebooks" with recipes collected over the years. Some had elementary ovens in their family dwellings, others used the ovens of the communal kitchen. This tradition produced many legendary bakers, and some of their notebooks were eventually published as cookbooks.

Fine cakes were once available only from a handful of bakeries run by professional pastry chefs. Every town had one or two famous ones, but as demand exceeded supply, home baking remained the norm. Regardless of ethnic origin, Israeli bakers, both professional and amateur, usually adhered to the traditions and recipes of Eastern and Central Europe (the Austro-Hungarian and German heritage). This was probably because skilled bakers from these countries were the founders of the local pastry industry and shaped the tastes and preferences of the people.

In later years, as food became more sophisticated and cosmopolitan, the selection of pastries expanded to include French and American influences. Middle Eastern ingredients also became more prominent: halva, tahini, phyllo dough, silan, dried dates and rose water were creatively fused with traditional European ingredients to produce cakes with unique local flair.

Today the Israeli pastry industry offers an overwhelming selection of cakes of every conceivable type, with home baking relegated to an enjoyable pastime. Specialty kitchen equipment shops proffer an infinite variety of appliances and gadgets. Israeli foodies, and baking enthusiasts in particular, can learn new recipes and techniques from dozens of cooking schools, magazines, TV shows and websites. And they do. The smell of cake still wafts out the windows of most households on Friday afternoons. Here is a really small sample of Shabbat cakes, which, in the spirit of this book, fuse East with West and tradition with innovation.

Citrus Semolina Cake

Semolina cakes are found throughout the Middle East and are popular in Jewish Sephardic kitchens. Called basbousa, safra, tishpishti or revani, they can be filled with dates, garnished with almonds, and can even be made with ground walnuts instead of, or in addition to, semolina. These crumbly dry cakes are doused with syrup immediately after baking, making them moist and very sweet.

The following is a slightly unorthodox version that contains freshly squeezed orange (or tangerine) juice and citrus marmalade, and is prepared with separated eggs for a light fluffy texture.

Ingredients (for a 25×30 cm/10×12 inch baking pan)

6 eggs, separated
100 g (31/2 oz, 1/2 cup) sugar
100 g (31/2 oz, 1 cup) ground coconut
140 g (5 oz, 1 cup) sifted flour
270 g (10 oz, 21/2 cups) semolina
25 g (1 oz, 11/2 tablespoons) ground almonds
20 g (2 small sachets, 4 teaspoons) baking powder
240 ml (81/2 fl oz, 1 cup) oil

360 ml (13 fl oz, 11/2 cup) freshly squeezed orange or tangerine juice
2 teaspoons grated orange zest
240 ml (81/2 fl oz, 1 cup) orange or lemon marmalade

The Syrup:
1 cup sugar
1 cup water

The Garnish:
Crushed almonds or coconut flakes

1. Preheat the oven to 180°C (350°F).
2. Using an electric mixer beat the egg whites with the sugar for 8 minutes until they hold stiff peaks.
3. Combine all the dry ingredients in a bowl: coconut, flour, semolina, ground almonds and baking powder.
4. Beat the egg yolks in a separate bowl, gradually adding the oil, juice, orange zest and marmalade.
5. Stir in the dry ingredients slowly until combined well. Gently fold in the peaked egg whites.
6. Pour the batter into a well-greased pan and bake for 30 minutes, until the cake turns golden and a toothpick comes out dry with a few crumbs adhering.
7. While the cake is in the oven prepare the syrup: Bring the water and sugar to a boil and simmer for 20 minutes. Cool slightly.
8. Take the cake out of the oven and pour on the syrup evenly. Cool completely and garnish with almonds or coconut.

Chocolate and Halva Coffeecake

Also known as babka or krantz, this old-world cake is a popular Shabbat offering in many households. The following version combines traditional chocolate filling and Middle Eastern halva, with an irresistible result. Strand halva is the most convenient to use for the filling but you can use regular halva (crumbled) as well. Another special ingredient is halva spread. Outside Israel it can be found in Middle Eastern groceries and kosher stores. If unavailable, prepare your own.

Ingredients (for 2 loaf pans)

The Dough:
560 g (1 lb 4 oz, 4 cups) bread flour
220 ml (8 oz, 1 cup less 1 tablespoon) water
50 g (2 oz) fresh yeast
100 g (31/2 oz, 1/2 cup) sugar
Pinch of salt
1 egg
2 egg yolks
1 teaspoon vanilla extract

100 g (31/2 oz) butter, softened
The Chocolate-Halva Filling:
200 g (7 oz, 1 cup) halva spread
250 g (9 oz) strand or regular halva, crumbled
200 g (7 oz, 1 cup) chocolate chips
Syrup (optional):
1 cup sugar
1 cup water

1. **Prepare the dough:** Place all ingredients except the butter in a mixer fitted with a kneading hook and knead for 7 minutes. Add butter and continue kneading for 5 minutes. The dough should be shiny and very soft. Transfer to a greased bowl, cover and allow to rise to twice the original size.

2. **Prepare the cakes:** Divide the dough in half and roll one piece on a well-floured surface to a 20×30 cm (9×12 inch) rectangle.

3. Spread the dough rectangle with a thin layer of halva spread. Sprinkle the strand or crumbled halva and chocolate chips and roll into a log. Slice the log lengthwise and braid the two pieces. Place in a loaf pan lined with baking paper and tuck in the edges of the cake so it fits snuggly into the pan. Repeat the process with the second piece of dough in the second pan. Allow to rise to twice the original size.

4. Preheat the oven to 180°C (350°F).

5. Bake the cakes for 35-40 minutes until deep golden-brown.

6. **While the cakes are in the oven prepare the syrup:** Bring the water and sugar to a boil and simmer for 20 minutes.

7. Brush the hot cakes with the syrup. They will keep fresh wrapped in foil for 3-4 days and can also be frozen.

Homemade Halva Spread

Halva is sweetened tahini.
Bring 200 ml (7 fl oz) of whipping cream to a boil. Pour over 200 g (7 oz) of chopped white chocolate. Wait for a minute and stir well until the chocolate dissolves. Add 200 g (7 oz) raw tahini and 1/4 cup water and mix thoroughly, to make a smooth spreadable paste.

Apple, Cinnamon and Walnut Cake

Every family has its recipe for a favorite apple cake. This one is attractive, perfumed with cinnamon, and has the added treat of crunchy walnuts.

Ingredients (for a 24 cm/10 inch diameter springform pan)

5 large baking apples, peeled and cored
Juice of half a lemon
280 g (10 oz, 2 cups) flour
1 teaspoon cinnamon
1 teaspoon baking soda
Pinch of salt
3 eggs
200 g (7 oz, 1 cup) sugar

180 ml (6 1/2 fl oz, 3/4 cup) oil
75 ml (3 fl oz, 5 tablespoons) brandy
or calvados
1 teaspoon vanilla extract
3/4 cup walnuts, coarsely chopped
For dusting:
2 tablespoons sugar
1 teaspoon cinnamon

1. Preheat the oven to 180°C (350°F).
2. Cut 3 apples into 1 cm (1/2 inch) dice. Slice the remaining two apples into 8 wedges each, sprinkle with lemon juice and set aside.
3. Sift the flour with cinnamon, baking soda and salt.
4. Using an electric mixer beat the eggs, sugar, brandy and vanilla extract until pale and thick, about 8 minutes.
5. Lower the speed and gradually add the oil and then the flour mixture.
6. Fold in the diced apples and chopped walnuts and pour the batter into a well-greased baking pan. Arrange the apple wedges in the center of the cake in a flower pattern. Combine sugar and cinnamon and sprinkle on top.
7. Bake for 60-70 minutes until the cake is golden and a toothpick comes out dry with a few crumbs adhering.
8. Cool for 10 minutes, release from the pan and cool completely on a rack.

Tahini Cookies

This may not sound too tempting but if you remember that halva is actually sweetened tahini, it starts to make sense. In fact, this confection is often called halva cookies even though it is made with raw tahini, which is more convenient for baking than halva. As opposed to the traditional Middle Eastern sweetmeat ma'amoul, tahini cookies are pretty much a modern invention. In the following version, tahini is enhanced with cinnamon and orange, a surprising and very effective combination.

Ingredients (for 50 about cookies)

250 g (9 oz) butter, softened
200 g (7 oz, 1 cup) sugar
2 teaspoons vanilla extract
1 teaspoon cinnamon
1 teaspoon grated orange zest
1/4 teaspoon salt
180 ml (61/2 fl oz, 3/4 cup) raw tahini

450 g (1 lb, 3 cups + 2 tablespoons) flour
10 g (1 small sachet, 2 teaspoons) baking powder
For Dusting:
3 tablespoons confectioners' sugar
1 heaping teaspoon cinnamon

1. In a mixer beat the butter and the sugar for 4-5 minutes until fluffy and creamy.
2. Lower the speed and add vanilla, cinnamon, salt, orange zest and tahini. Beat to a smooth consistency. Add the flour and baking powder and process to a smooth and malleable dough. Cover and refrigerate for one hour.
3. Preheat the oven to 180°C (350°F).
4. Mix the confectioners' sugar with cinnamon in a small bowl.
5. Pinch small pieces off the dough and roll balls the size of large olives. Roll the balls in the sugar-cinnamon mixture.
6. Arrange the cookies on a tray lined with baking paper, spacing them. Bake for 15 minutes. The cookies should remain light colored. Don't touch them until they cool completely or they will crumble. Store in an airtight jar.

Ma'amoul

Delicious, delicate, date-filled cookies that are served with tea or coffee throughout the Middle East. The characteristic grooved pattern is created by a special ma'amoul utensil that looks like a tweezer, but you can get a similar effect with a fork.

Ingredients (for about 50 cookies)

The Filling:
500 g (1 lb 2 oz) pressed pitted dates (see explanation on p. 280)
1 teaspoon cinnamon
5 drops orange blossom water
200 g (7 oz) butter, softened
The Dough:
560 g (1 lb 4 oz, 4 cups) bread flour
100 g (31/2 oz, 1 cup)

semolina
10 g (1 small sachet, 2 teaspoons) baking powder
1 teaspoon vanilla extract
200 g (7 oz) butter
120 ml (4 oz, 1/2 cup) oil
50 g (2 oz) sugar
5 drops orange blossom water
Confectioners' sugar for dusting

1. Preheat the oven to 180°C (350°F).
2. **Prepare the filling:** Combine all the ingredients and mix thoroughly. Roll about fifty balls the size of large olives.
3. **Prepare the dough:** Fit a mixer with a kneading hook and knead the ingredients for about 3 minutes to a smooth dough.
4. **Prepare the cookies:** Pinch small pieces off the dough and roll balls twice the size of the date balls. Flatten the ball on the palm of your hand. Place a date ball in the center and reshape into a ball. Create grooves with a special utensil or a fork.
5. Arrange the cookies on a tray lined with baking paper, spacing them, and bake for 20 minutes. Remove from the oven before the cookies turn golden.
6. Dust with confectioners' sugar while the cookies are still warm (the sugar will adhere better), cool and store in an airtight jar.

Coffee

Cafés are everywhere — in shopping malls, on seaside promenades, commercial streets and neighborhood lanes, and are packed with patrons ranging from moms with strollers to businessmen with laptops. Coffee is the drink of choice, be it instant, iced, black (with cardamom), or today's preference — Italian style espresso or cappuccino. Strange as it may sound, Tel Aviv is a better place for coffee than most European capitals and its beautiful cafés are a source of pride to the locals. A few very successful chains dominate the market, but happily there are still plenty of privately owned neighborhood cafés that retain their unique personality and attract diverse clienteles.

The first new-wave espresso bars arrived on the local food scene in the late eighties, and in a few years became an inseparable part of the cityscape. The owners were quick to realize that the coffee may well be Italian, but the dynamics must be adapted to the local lifestyle. Rather than have a quick coffee standing up or as a take-out, patrons prefer to sit down, relax, maybe order something to eat. Baked goods and sandwiches are not enough, and most cafés now serve light meals. Some are even better known for their food than their coffee. On the other hand, it is perfectly acceptable to linger for hours over a single cup of espresso, and no waiter would dream of hurrying you up.

Cheese
Between White, Yellow and Salty

Not so many years ago the local cheese scene could be summarized in three simple notions: *gvina levana* (white cheese), *gvina tzehuba* (yellow cheese) and *gvina melucha* (salty cheese). Not that the local dairy industry was backward. Quite the opposite. The yield of local milk cows is among the highest in the world and Israelis rightly pride themselves on the excellence of the fresh dairy products. Local cottage cheese is one of the best in the world, and other fresh cheese and soured milk products (kefir, yogurt, leben, etc.) are equally delicious. The family of salt-brined cheeses (*gvina melucha*), typical to the Mediterranean, also boasts some wonderful members (see the story of Safed Cheese on p. 220).

The weakest link was *gvina tzehuba*, yellow cheese, a collective name given to all hard and semi-hard cheeses. Not that there were that many. A handful of mild-tasting processed cheeses was all that grocery stores and supermarkets had to offer. Most of the population was quite happy with this basic selection, and used it for toast, sandwiches, and occasionally for baking. Plates of sophisticated ripened cheeses to be savored with fine wine were foreign notions. Imported cheeses were virtually nonexistent due to restrictive trade policies. Gourmet cheese was something one brought back from Paris or Rome. Indeed, chefs would smuggle slabs of Parmesan in suitcases for use in their kitchens.

Then, in the early 1980s, the formative decade that changed the face of local gastronomy, rumors began to circulate of delicious handmade cheeses produced on small privately-owned farms. The concept was novel and intriguing. Up until then all dairy products were produced by large industrial ▷

Safed Cheese

When fresh it is soft, silky and delicately salty. When aged it is rock hard, very salty and perfect for grating and cooking. Safed cheese, named after the ancient holy city of Safed where it was invented, is one of the few local indigenous cheeses. Its round shape and uneven exterior are created when the curds are placed in round wicker baskets to drain the whey. Similar cheeses have been produced around the Middle East and Mediterranean for centuries.

The birthplace of this unique cheese is Hameiri Dairy, founded by Meir Arzoni, who came to Safed from Iran in 1840 to help rebuild the town following the disastrous earthquake of 1837. Arzoni, a jeweler by training, quickly realized there was no demand for his trade and began producing cheese according to a family recipe, using sheep and goat milk purchased from local shepherds. Six generations later, the dairy is still situated in the old family home and run by two direct descendants of the founder. Adhering to established cheese-making traditions and insisting on fresh sheep and goat milk, Hameiri Dairy (the country's first commercial dairy) still produces the original Safed cheese, but is even more famous for its silky, rich, Balkan-style Brinza cheese. Immigrants who arrived from Bulgaria in the early 1950s were quick to adopt this cheese so similar to one from the old country, and from that time on it came to be known simply as Bulgarian cheese.

In the early 1980s rumors began to circulate of delicious handmade cheeses produced on small privately-owned farms. The concept was novel and intriguing.

◁ concerns, led by the the kibbutz movement giant Tnuva. Suddenly there were new players on the field. Foodies and chefs began making trips to these farms, paying premium prices for handmade goat and sheep milk cheeses of the kind found in rural France, Spain and Italy. It was love at first sight. Picturesque locations and tours of the dairy, tastings and light meals made the experience even more pleasurable.

Three farms pioneered artisan cheese-making in Israel. Curiously, all three started producing almost simultaneously between 1980 and 1981, came to cheese making by accident, and are doing very well to this day.

Avinoam and Michal Brakin were farmers in the Jezreel Valley Kefar Yehezkiel cooperative. A volunteer working at their farm told them about her experience making goat cheese in the French Pyrenees and suggested they do the same with the milk from their goat herd. Avinoam and Michal went off to France for a month-long tour of rural cheese farms, a journey that changed their lives. They founded the Barkanit dairy farm, today one of the leading boutique goat cheese producers in the country.

Drora and Amiram Ovrutski built the beautiful Ein Kammonim farm in the Lower Galilee with a plan to raise Barbary ducks. The venture failed, leaving the family in deep debt. Rather than give up they turned their efforts to cultivating olive groves and raising goats for milk. Drora, a gifted painter, proved to be equally talented as a cheese maker. Amiram, later joined by his children, tended the animals and ran the farm. Today, Ein Kammonim, like Barkanit, is one of the largest and most successful handmade cheese producers in the country.

Shay Seltser left Jerusalem and a scientific career in Botany in search of a quiet life close to nature on an isolated farm high in the Jerusalem hills. Brother Vasilius, a monk from the nearby St. John in the Desert Monastery, gave him his first lessons in making cheese. With his unique combination of scientific curiosity and new-age romanticism, Shay threw himself wholeheartedly into the new venture. Today his farm is a must-stop for visiting chefs and culinary luminaries, and his cheeses are world-class by any standard.   ▷

Shay Seltser and his creation

Neot Midbar Dairy Farm in the Negev Desert

As opposed to traditional farms in rural Europe, which specialize in one or two cheeses based on age-old traditional recipes, Israeli farms each produce a large variety of cheeses, much like their counterparts in the United States and Australia.

◁ These pioneers paved the way for more boutique cheese producers who were quick to follow the trend. The lovely Chalav Eem Haruach in the Lower Galilee operates without electricity and is strictly organic. Its Sardinian-style pecorino and ricotta are pure delight. Not far from there, at Hanoked Farm with its beautiful cellars and renovated visitors center, Danny Barzilay turns out a variety of extremely well-made, full-flavored goat and sheep cheeses. The Rom Farm, also in the lower Galilee, is famous for its fresh organic goat milk cheeses and yogurts.

The largest concentration of boutique cheese farms is in the Galilee, but there are quite a few notable ones in central Israel, such as Tal in Beer-Yacov, Har Haruach near Jerusalem, and Bitzaron near Rehovot, which specializes in buffalo milk mozarella. A few cheese producers have even sprung up in the heart of the Negev desert, a prominent one being Kornmehl Dairy.

The majority of boutique cheeses in Israel are made from goat milk, and the rest from sheep and cow milk. Most producers use the milk from their own herds, and many are organic. As opposed to traditional cheese farms in rural Europe, which specialize in one or two cheeses based on age-old traditional recipes, these Israeli farms each produce a large variety of cheeses, much like their counterparts in the United States and Australia.

The quantities produced by these farms are minute compared to the big industrial firms, but their influence far exceeds the sales figures. Large producers rose to the challenge and added new sophisticated items to their product lines. Chefs and home cooks were delighted with the infinite uses of fine goat and sheep cheeses in cooking and baking. The average family still buys yellow cheese for everyday use, but gourmet cheeses are a popular, sought-after treat and a source of local culinary pride.

Gvina Levana

Most Israelis do not refer to soft white cheese (*gvina levana*) by its various trade names. Instead, they refer to it by its fat content: nine percent and five percent. Eaten with a teaspoon, mixed with fruit or vegetable salad, spread on bread or crackers, and used in a variety of pies and pastries, this is one of the most in-demand foods in Israel.

Interestingly, the people responsible for introducing this all-Israeli cheese to the region were members of a German Christian society, the Templers. The Temple Society (no connection to the Order of the Templar Knights) was established in 1861 by Christoph Hoffmann, who believed that his followers should settle in the Land of Israel in order to prepare for the second coming of Christ. The Templers first came here in 1868, shortly before the beginning of Zionist resettlement, when the area was still part of the Ottoman Empire. These hard-working, god-fearing settlers established several urban and rural settlements (notably in Jerusalem, Jaffa and Haifa) and engaged in commerce and agriculture. They built impressive churches, community halls, schools and houses in the best tradition of German architecture. They grew and exported Jaffa oranges and were responsible for introducing the domesticated honeybee, modern horse-drawn carriages, and, most importantly, modern dairy farming based on cow milk. Local dairy products at the time came entirely from sheep and goat milk.

With the advent of Zionist immigration and the growing demand for milk and dairy products, the Templers became the primary suppliers of dairy products to the Jews of Palestine.

When unable to deliver their fresh milk to the market, they made butter and soured milk products rather than let the milk go to waste. The fresh soft cheese was modeled after Quark, a popular product in Central Europe (known in German as Weißkäse, literally white cheese).

By the mid-1930s the number of Jewish dairies rose and the Templers' dairy farms lost their supremacy. In addition, many Templers pledged their allegiance to the Nazi regime in Germany, and the Jewish community of Palestine boycotted all Templer goods and services. To utilize the huge amounts of unwanted milk, the Templers established two modern dairies and sold their products mainly to the British Army. By the early 1940s, the British authorities had the Templers of Palestine (whom they suspected of aiding the Germans) interred and subsequently deported, first to Cyprus and finally to Australia. They were never allowed to return.

Following the establishment of the State of Israel, dairy farming became a major sector of Israeli agriculture, and the huge amounts of milk being supplied by the moshav and kibbutz settlements were used to make dairy products, mainly soft white cheese. Inexpensive, simple to produce and nutritious, this cheese soon became an important staple in the years of austerity and rationing. Later on it was perfected and now has a smoother creamier texture.

Admittedly, soft white cheese was not invented in Israel, but Israelis are probably its most devout consumers worldwide. This status and its colorful local history make *gvina levana* a uniquely Israeli food product. ▷

The kidding season at Ein Kammonim Dairy Farm in the Galilee

holidays

Rosh Hashanah

Summer still hangs in the air, the school year has just begun, and Israelis are getting ready to welcome Rosh Hashanah, the Jewish New Year that is celebrated during September/ October according to the Jewish calendar. Even for those whose daily lives are governed by the January to December calendar, Rosh Hashanah is a major event: awe-inspiring yet full of hope, an occasion for a festive family reunion featuring a menu laden with symbolism.

Shana Tova ve Metuka ("May you have a good and sweet year") is the traditional greeting. Indeed, sweetness is the main motif of the New Year dinner, which begins with apples dipped in honey and ends with honey cake. The traditional braided Sabbath challah gives way to a round Rosh Hashanah challah that symbolizes the cycle of life. Fish dishes symbolizing abundance are mandatory and the head of the fish stands for the desire to "be the head rather than the tail". The seeds of the pomegranate symbolize the 613 commandments of the Torah. Carrot slices represent gold coins, embodying the wish for a prosperous year, and the list goes on and on.

The following selection of Rosh Hashanah foods highlights the festive and optimistic nature of this holiday — traditional Ashkenazi and Sephardic fish dishes, a sumptous meat casserole, and of course the luscious honey cake.

No other Jewish dish has been the subject of so much scorn, mockery and praise as gefilte fish. Firstly, it is made of carp, and who in their right mind would consider this fat, bland, bony fish for the table? Secondly, the proper Jewish-Polish recipe calls for sugar. Sweet fish? The usual response would be a polite "No, thank you". Actually, the sweetness of gefilte fish is relative. Polish Jews like it quite sweet, Hungarian and Lithuanian Jews spice it up with pepper, while Russian Jews balance the sugar with salt. And, finally, there is the jellied aspic, rich and flavorful but off-putting for many people. But all these objections fly right out the window the minute you taste lovingly prepared gefilte fish. Gefilte means stuffed in Yiddish. One fish is sliced right across and the cavity in the slices is stuffed with the ground meat of another fish. Today most cooks prefer to prepare round, flat fish patties. Carp is the classic choice, but other fatty freshwater fish like whitefish or pike can be used as well. The horseradish dip (chrain) that accompanies the fish endows it with everything it lacks: a violet red color and fierce spiciness.

Dadi's Gefilte Fish
Dadi Shaulski, Mul Eden, Tel Aviv

Dadi learned to make gefilte fish and other Ashkenazi specialties from her Russian grandmothers. She doesn't like it on the sweet side, but you can change the sugar-salt-pepper ratio according to taste. She adds fried carrots and onions to the fish, which give flavor and a golden hue to the patties. Ask your fishmonger to fillet the fish, and put the skins, bones and heads in a separate bag. The fish should be ground in a meat grinder; if you don't have one at home, ask the fishmonger to grind it for you. In this case the rest of the ingredients for the patties should be chopped in a food processor and mixed thoroughly with the ground fish.

Ingredients (makes 25 fish patties)

For the Fish Patties:
1 kg (2 lb 4 oz) filleted carp, without skin (net weight)
Oil for frying
1 large onion, chopped coarsely
2 carrots, chopped coarsely
3-4 eggs
1/3 cup breadcrumbs (or matzo meal for Passover)
3/4 tablespoon salt
2 tablespoons sugar (or more, to taste)
1 teaspoon ground white pepper

For the Fish Stock:
1-2 carp heads, halved, washed thoroughly and gills removed
Skins and bones from the filleted carp
4 carrots
2 large onions, whole
2 tablespoons salt
1/2 teaspoon white peppercorns
3-4 tablespoons sugar
3 bay leaves
6 allspice berries

To Serve:
Chrain (horseradish sauce, p. 232)

1. **Prepare the fish patties:** Heat the oil in a skillet and fry the carrots and onions until the onions turn translucent.
2. In a meat grinder, grind the fish together with the onions and carrots. Mix with the other ingredients for the fish patties and season. If you are using ground fish and don't have a meat grinder, chop the fried carrots and onions finely in a food processor and mix with the rest of the ingredients.
3. **Prepare the fish stock:** Put all the ingredients in a wide saucepan, add about 2 liters (2 quarts) water, to cover the contents, and bring to a simmer.
4. With wet hands, form elongated or round patties and slide carefully into the saucepan. Partly cover the saucepan (the smell is overpowering so open a window). Simmer for two hours, making sure the fish patties remain covered by the stock.
5. Cool the stock slightly and strain. Save the carrots for garnishing. Cover the fish with the stock and refrigerate overnight, during which time the stock should jell.
6. Serve the fish patties garnished with cooked carrot slices and some of the jelly.

Chrain — Horseradish Sauce for Gefilte Fish

The ratio of horseradish to beetroots may change according to personal preference and the quality of the ingredients — beetroots tend to be sweeter in winter, while young horseradish root is especially hot.

Ingredients (about 1 cup)
500 g (1 lb 2 oz) horseradish root, peeled
1 kg (2 lb 4 oz) beetroots, peeled
1/4 cup white vinegar

1-2 teaspoons sugar
1/2 teaspoon salt

1. Soak the horseradish root in water for 20 minutes. Cut it into 3-4 chunks and grind finely in the food processor. Set aside.
2. Grate the beetroots finely in the food processor.
3. Mix most of the ground horseradish with the ground beetroots and taste. If it's not hot enough, add more horseradish.
4. Mix 1/4 cup water with vinegar, salt and sugar. Stir well until the sugar and salt dissolve. Add the liquid gradually to the horseradish and beetroots to the desired consistency. Taste and adjust seasoning. Serve immediately or refrigerate in a sealed jar for a few days.

Moroccan-style Hot Fish

Guy Peretz, Gazpacho, Holiday Inn, Ashkelon

Chunks of fine saltwater fish (traditionally grouper) are cooked casserole-style with hot peppers and garlic. No holiday dinner in a Jewish Moroccan household is complete without it.

Ingredients (serves 8)
8 portion-sized (about 180 g, 6 oz) chunks of grouper or other saltwater fish
4 hot red peppers, cut into strips
2 sweet red peppers, cut into strips
20 cloves garlic, peeled
1 cup fresh parsley, chopped coarsely

1 cup fresh coriander, chopped coarsely
The Seasoning Mix:
8 tablespoons paprika
Salt
1 cup olive oil

1. Line a wide saucepan with the peppers and herbs.
2. Mix the ingredients of the seasoning mix. Dip the fish chunks in the mix and arrange in the saucepan. Mix the remaining seasoning mix with the garlic and 3-4 cups of water and pour over the fish.
3. Cook for 10-15 minutes (depending on the size of the fish chunks) over a high heat, lower the heat, cover and continue cooking for another 15 minutes until the sauce thickens.

Baked Pumpkin Jam
with Cinnamon and Ginger

Guy Peretz, Gazpacho, Holiday Inn, Ashkelon

A delicious sweet side dish from Moroccan Jewish cuisine, traditionally served on a bed of couscous at Rosh Hashanah dinner.

Ingredients (serves 6-8)

500 g (1 lb 2 oz) pumpkin (net weight), peeled and cut into 2-3 cm (1 inch) cubes
1 large onion, sliced into half rings
2 tablespoons olive oil
200 g (7 oz, 1/2 cup) sugar

1/2 teaspoon cinnamon
1/2 teaspoon fresh ginger, chopped
3 thyme sprigs
To serve:
1/2 kg (1 lb 2 oz) instant couscous

1. Fry the onions in the olive oil, add the sugar and stir until it dissolves. Add the spices and mix together.
2. Preheat the oven to 160°C (310°F).
3. Put the pumpkin on a tray lined with baking paper. Pour the onion mixture on top and bake for about 15 minutes until the pumpkin is tender and caramel colored.
4. **To serve:** Prepare the couscous according to the manufacturer's instructions. Arrange in a heap on a large serving plate and garnish with the pumpkin.

Lamb and Quince Casserole

Yehiel Filosof, Balkan Restaurant, Jaffa

A traditional lamb casserole for Rosh Hashanah that features quince, the autumn fruit Bulgarian Jewish cooks love.

Ingredients (serves 6-8)

1 kg (2 lb 4 oz) lamb cut into large cubes
4 tablespoons oil
3 large quinces, peeled, cored and cut into 6 wedges each

Salt and freshly ground black pepper
1 level teaspoon sweet paprika
4-5 teaspoons sugar

1. Heat the oil in a large saucepan and brown the meat. Cover with boiling water, put on the lid and cook for an hour or more, until the meat is tender and almost ready to eat.
2. Add the quince wedges, season and cook for another 10 minutes.
3. In the meantime, dissolve the sugar and 2-3 tablespoons water in a frying pan and cook to a light-colored caramel. Add some of the lamb cooking liquid to the caramel and stir well. Pour the caramel into the saucepan and cook for another 10 minutes, until the lamb is completely tender and the quince wedges are soft but retain their shape. Serve with steamed rice.

Magical Honey Cake

"Do you have a really good recipe for a honey cake?" This is a standard query of the pre-Rosh Hashanah rush. The following recipe was given to us by an enthusiastic amateur cook, Dalia Zarchiya, and has been our favorite for years. Pay attention: the cake should "mature" for seven days before serving.

Ingredients (for 3 loaf pans)

880 g (2 lb, 6 cups + 3 tablespoons) flour
300 g (101/2 oz, 11/2 cups) sugar
2 heaping teaspoons cinnamon
500 g (1 lb 2 oz, 11/2 cups) honey
240 ml (81/2 fl oz, 1 cup) oil

4 eggs
2 tablespoons instant coffee
2 level teaspoons baking soda
1/3 cup raisins
1/2 cup walnuts, chopped

1. Preheat the oven to 170°C (325°F).
2. Combine the flour, sugar and cinnamon in a bowl. Add the honey, oil and eggs and beat into a smooth batter with a whisk or a mixer.
3. Dissolve the instant coffee in 1 cup of boiling water. Stir the baking soda and then the coffee into the batter. Gently fold in the raisins and walnuts.
4. Pour the batter into greased pans and bake for about 45 minutes, until the top of the cake is dark brown and a toothpick comes out dry with a few crumbs adhering.
5. Allow the cakes to cool completely, wrap with aluminum foil and place in a cool, dry place (not in the refrigerator) to mature for 7 days.

Variation: If you don't like the taste of coffee in your honey cake, replace it with one cup of strong dark tea.

Hanukkah

Hanukkah celebrates the victory of the inferior army of the Jews over the Greeks and the subsequent rededication of The Temple in 165 BCE. According to legend, when the victorious Maccabees liberated Jerusalem and reentered The Temple, they discovered that everything had been desecrated, including the oil used to fuel the eternal flame of the holy Menorah (the seven-branched candelabra). All they could find was one small cruse of holy oil, which miraculously kept the Menorah alight for eight days instead of only one.

This story gave rise to the two major customs of the holiday: the kindling of a Menorah over eight nights and the eating of foods deep-fried in oil. Both customs, along with a week-long school break, make this winter holiday a favorite of children. At one time there may have been only a single Hanukkah Menorah in the home, the classroom, or even an entire community. Today every youngster makes his own Menorah and insists on lighting it. Typical children's Hanukkah parties feature scores of Menorahs, each lit by its maker, with parents closely monitoring the festive but potentially dangerous ceremony.

The two most popular Hanukkah foods are pancakes (*latkes* in Yiddish, *levivot* in Hebrew) and doughnuts (*bimuelos* in Ladino, *ponchikes* in Yiddish, *sufganiyot* in Hebrew). Hanukkah pancakes are made from a variety of ingredients, from traditional potatoes and cheese, to corn, spinach, zucchinis and apples, to yams and herbs. Hanukkah doughnuts are usually made from yeast-based dough, cake batter or lighter batters. These eagerly-anticipated doughnuts appear in stores and bakeries several weeks before Hanukkah and disappear as soon as the holiday is over. They may be getting smaller due to 21st Century concerns over calorie counts, but fillings and toppings are becoming ever more creative.

Making ahead: After forming the doughnuts (step 6), place them on a tray lined with baking paper, wrap the tray in a plastic bag and freeze. Defrost for 8 hours in the refrigerator and continue according to the recipe (from step 7).

Sufganiyot — Hanukkah Doughnuts

Hans Bertele, Gaya Patisserie Shop, Petach Tikvah

Preparing doughnuts at home takes some motivation. So if you decide to go to the trouble make a lot, freeze them and fry some each day.

Ingredients (for 30 regular doughnuts or 50 mini-doughnuts)

The Dough:
50 g (2 oz) fresh yeast
160 ml (51/2 fl oz, 2/3 cup) lukewarm milk
1 kg (2 lb 4 oz, 7 cups) flour
160 g (51/2 oz, 3/4 cup + 1 tablespoon) sugar
10 g (2 teaspoons) salt
8 eggs
1 teaspoon vanilla extract
The zest of half a lemon

The zest of half an orange
45 ml (3 tablespoons) rum or brandy
160 g (6 oz) soft butter

For Frying:
Sunflower oil (burns slowly and has no aftertaste), for deep-frying

The Filling:
1 cup strawberry jam

To Serve:
Confectioners' sugar

1. Dissolve the yeast in 1/4 cup milk.
2. Put the flour, sugar, salt, eggs, vanilla extract, citrus zest, rum or brandy, and the remaining milk in a mixer bowl fitted with a kneading hook. Add the dissolved yeast and knead for 5 minutes.
3. Add the butter gradually and continue kneading for 10 minutes at medium speed, until the dough is smooth.
4. Sprinkle some flour over the dough in the bowl, cover with a moist towel and allow to rest for 20-30 minutes.
5. Knead the dough for another minute, form a smooth ball (it should weigh about 1.8 kg/4 lb at this point), and place on a work surface, preferably wood, sprinkled with flour. Cover with a moist towel and allow to rise for 15-20 minutes.
6. Divide the dough into 30 doughnuts (or 50 mini-doughnuts) and arrange, evenly spaced, on greased baking pans sprinkled with flour.
7. Transfer the pans to a warm oven preheated to 40-45°C (about 110°F). Place a saucepan with boiling water at the bottom of the oven to provide the dough with the necessary moisture. Allow the doughnuts to rise in the warm oven until they double in size.
8. Heat the oil for deep-frying to 190°C (375°F).
9. Make sure there is no excess flour on the doughnuts, which can burn and cloud the oil, and fry the doughnuts in batches. Place them in the hot oil with the bottom (the side on which the doughnut was resting) facing up. The dome (top side) will develop a crust while the bottom will swell up slightly and the doughnut will take on a perfect round shape. Fry for about 2 minutes on each side, until golden-brown. Taste the first doughnut to be sure it has been fried properly; if it's brown on the outside and still moist and sticky on the inside, the oil is too hot.
10. Arrange the doughnuts on a rack to allow the excess oil to drip.
11. **To fill the doughnuts:** Use a special syringe or a pastry bag with a long nozzle. Puncture the doughnut in the center, and press to release the filling. If the jam is too thick mix in a little water. Sprinkle with confectioners' sugar and serve.

Hanukkah at Roladin Bakery, Tel Aviv
Scores of toppings and fillings, and mini-doughnuts for the guilty conscience

Ashkenazi Potato Latkes

These delicious potato pancakes are a highlight of Hanukkah get-togethers.

Ingredients (makes 25 pancakes)

5 potatoes, grated coarsely
2 onions, grated finely
1 carrot, grated coarsely (optional)
3 eggs

3 tablespoons breadcrumbs
Salt and freshly ground black pepper
Pinch of grated nutmeg
Oil for frying

1. Thoroughly squeeze the grated potatoes, onions and carrots and mix. Add the eggs, breadcrumbs and spices and mix again.
2. Heat the oil in a frying pan. Heap spoonfuls of the mix into the pan and pat them down to form pancakes. Fry for 2 minutes, turn over and fry for another minute until golden. Drain on paper towel and serve hot.

Balkan Potato and Leek Pancakes

Crisp and rich, these pancakes are made from potato purée mixed with leeks.

Ingredients (makes 25 pancakes)

2 leeks (white part only), chopped
Oil for frying
5 potatoes
Salt and freshly ground black pepper

For the Crust:
Flour
3 eggs, beaten

1. Cook the potatoes in their jackets in boiling water until they are tender. Cool slightly, peel and mash.
2. Heat oil in a frying pan. Add the chopped leeks and fry for 8 minutes or until tender and golden.
3. Mix the fried leeks with the potato purée and season with salt and pepper. Roll the mix into a sausage and cut into 2 cm (3/4 inch) thick slices.
4. Heat more oil in a clean frying pan. Dip the slices in flour and then in egg and fry 2 minutes on each side, until golden. Remove the pancakes from the pan, drain on paper towel and serve hot.

Blossoming almond trees, the first sign of Spring,
are the symbol of Tu bi'Shvat

Tu bi'Shvat

Originally not a festival at all, Tu bi'Shvat was merely a date on the Jewish calendar, literally "the 15th day of Shvat". This was the date on which the age of trees was calculated for the purposes of tithing and taxing. Thus, in Judaic sources it came to be known as the New Year for the Trees. In Biblical times, Tu bi'Shvat was the day farmers brought the first fruits of their trees to The Temple in Jerusalem. When The Temple was destroyed and the Jewish People were exiled from the Land of Israel, Tu bi'Shvat lost much of its original significance, only to be rediscovered in the Middle Ages by Jewish mystics who imbued it with deeper symbolic meaning. Tu bi'Shvat Seder Meal was established by the Kabbalists of Safed, modeled after the Passover Seder and featuring the seven species of the Land of Israel: wheat, barley, vines, figs, pomegranates, olive oil and dates, the staples of the Biblical Period. The custom spread across the Diaspora and for generations Jews all over the world marked the day by eating fruits from the Land of Israel, mainly dried ones like figs and dates, raisins and almonds. Thus, Tu bi'Shvat took on another meaning: the longing for the Promised Land.

The holiday was further transformed in modern Israel and it is now a day on which tree saplings are planted. As far as food is concerned — every Jewish holiday must have some culinary aspect — Israelis still feast on dried fruit, even though fresh fruits abound even at the height of winter.

Tu bi'Shvat Cake

Lots and lots of dried fruits and nuts and just a little bit of dough to hold them all together. The choice of fruit is all yours, the more the merrier. Just remember to combine different colors to make the cake more attractive. This dense, juicy, not overly sweet cake will keep for a long time.

Dried fruit stalls in Tel Aviv Lewinsky Market

Ingredients (for 1 loaf pan)

60 g (2 oz, 7 tablespoons) flour
60 g (2 oz, 7 tablespoons) sugar
3 eggs
200 g (7 oz) assorted dried fruits (prunes, apricots, raisins, figs, papaya, cranberries)

200 g (7 oz) assorted nuts (walnuts, pecans, hazelnuts, almonds)
1/2 teaspoon cinnamon
1/4 teaspoon nutmeg
Small pinch of ground cloves

1. Preheat oven to 150°C (300°F).
2. Mix flour, sugar, eggs and spices.
3. Chop larger dried fruits (apricots, prunes, papaya) coarsely. Add them with the rest of the fruits and the nuts to the dough and mix thoroughly.
4. Transfer to a greased loaf pan and bake for 11/2 hours, until the cake is deep golden-brown.
5. Cool completely and slice very thin with a bread knife, but only what you plan to serve. The unsliced cake keeps better.

Chocolate and Dried Fruit Petit Fours

Delicious sweets prepared in under five minutes.

Ingredients (makes 25 petit fours)

200 g (7 oz) bittersweet chocolate, chopped
60 g (2 oz) butter
300 g (10 oz) assorted dried fruits and nuts (raisins, figs and apricots; walnuts, hazelnuts and pecans), chopped finely

1. Melt the chocolate and butter in a double boiler or in a microwave oven. Stir well until smooth.
2. Mix the melted chocolate with the dried fruits and nuts.
3. Ladle 2-3 teaspoons of the mixture into small paper baking cups and freeze for 1/2 hour before serving.

Dried Fruit Compote

Simple, refreshing and delicious, this is the traditional ending to a rich Shabbat dinner or any other festive meal. Feel free to alter the ratio of the fruits according to personal preference. Remember though to go easy on the apple rings as they swell considerably during cooking.

Ingredients (serves 6-8)

1 cup dried apricots
1 cup prunes, with pits (to maintain the shape)
1/2 cup dried apple rings

3/4 cup raisins
1/2 cup sugar
1 cinnamon stick
Half a lemon

1. Put the ingredients in a large saucepan. Add water to twice the level of the fruit.
2. Bring to a boil, lower the heat and cook for about 30 minutes. Adjust the seasoning, adding sugar if you like it sweeter.
3. Refrigerate and serve well chilled.

Sephardic Dried Fruit and Nut Spoon Sweet

A sinfully rich combination of deep-fried dried fruits, nuts and honey, perfumed with orange blossom water. Serve it with tea or spoon some over yogurt and ice cream.

Ingredients (makes 1 liter jar)

450 g (1 lb) assorted dried fruits (prunes, dates, figs, pineapples, apricots, raisins)
250 g (9 oz) assorted nuts (pecans, walnuts, almonds, hazelnuts, cashews)

Oil for deep-frying
350 g (12 oz) honey
5 drops orange blossom water

1. Heat the oil for deep-frying to medium heat.
2. Cut the larger fruits into small-cubes. Fry the fruits and the nuts in batches in hot oil for about 1 minute. Be careful not to scorch the fruit. Transfer with a slotted spoon to a bowl.
3. Pour the honey into the bowl, add orange blossom water and mix thoroughly. Cool to room temperature and serve. It will keep for a long time in the refrigerator. Before serving, heat for 20-30 seconds in the microwave oven.

Passover

The weeks preceding the Passover holiday are busy and hectic. First and foremost, according to the Jewish religious custom, homes must be cleansed of every last bit of *hametz* — leavened foods and beverages including pastry and beer, which are strictly forbidden during Passover. Most nonobservant households also seize the opportunity to launch that once-a-year Spring cleaning. In addition, gifts have to be purchased, visits with relatives and friends scheduled, family quarrels reconciled, guests invited, groceries bought, and elaborate meals planned and cooked, starting with the ritual Seder Night dinner.

And yet, practically every Israeli has fond memories of past Passover holidays, especially childhood ones. The weeklong national holiday gives people the opportunity to travel around the country and abroad, visit friends and relatives, and generally enjoy the glories of springtime. And then there is the traditional Seder meal — the ritual dinner and occasion for an elaborate family reunion, which brings us back to food, arguably the trickiest part of the Passover celebrations. Certain food categories are untouchable — not just all leavened pastry but many grains and legumes as well. In short, a completely different menu is called for.

Over the centuries, numerous dishes have been developed and a host of ingenious substitutes for the usual fare have evolved to take the place of the forbidden ingredients. Some of these dishes are so good they deserve to be savored throughout the year. Here are a few of our favorites.

Green Passover Chicken Soup with Dumplings

Clear chicken soup with matzo dumplings (knedlach) is the most popular starter for the Seder meal and one of the few Ashkenazi dishes to be adopted in practically every Israeli household. The following recipe takes a few liberties with this classic: the dumplings are enhanced with aromatic spices and cooked in a soup that welcomes the green vegetables of Spring. If you prefer to stick to tradition, serve the dumplings in a clear chicken soup (p. 194).

Ingredients (serves 8-10)

1 kg (2 lb 4 oz) chicken and turkey parts and bones
2 onions, chopped
1 celery root, diced
3 celery stalks, diced
3 tablespoons oil
1/3 cup dill, chopped
1/3 cup fresh coriander, chopped
1/3 cup fresh parsley, chopped
1/2 kg (1 lb 2 oz) fresh or frozen broad (fava) beans
2 potatoes, diced

2 leeks, white part only, sliced
1 level tablespoon turmeric (optional)
Salt and freshly ground white pepper

The Chicken Knedlach (Dumplings):
250 g (9 oz) chicken breast, ground
1 cup matzo flour
2 eggs
2 tablespoons oil
2 cloves garlic, crushed
3 tablespoons fresh coriander, chopped
Salt and freshly ground white pepper
1/2 cup chicken stock or water

1. **Prepare the soup:** Brown the bones with the onions and celery root and stalks in a saucepan with some oil. Add 3 liters (3 quarts) of water, the dill, coriander and parsley. Bring to a boil and cook for about one hour. Strain and retain the broth.
2. Add the beans, potatoes and leeks to the broth and bring to a boil. Season and cook for 45 minutes over a low-medium heat until the vegetables are tender.
3. **Prepare the dumplings:** Mix the ingredients and refrigerate for 30 minutes.
4. **Before serving:** Bring the soup to a boil, form small balls of the dumpling mixture using two spoons or your hands, and slide into the boiling soup. Cook for 20 minutes and serve.

Charred Artichoke Bottoms with Fish Tartare and Argan Oil

Yaniv Gur Ariye, Touch Food Cooking School, Raanana

Artichokes are a popular Spring vegetable, often served at the Seder table. In this recipe, artichoke bottoms are baked briefly in the oven to give them that special charred taste, then filled with fish tartare perfumed with argan oil. Produced from the fruit of the argan tree, this exotic Moroccan ingredient has become very trendy and is now used worldwide. If unavailable, use olive oil.

Ingredients (serves 8)

The Sauce:
5 tomatoes
2 red peppers
2 cloves garlic
Half a fresh red hot pepper
2 tablespoons sherry vinegar
3 tablespoons argan oil (or olive oil)
Salt

The Tartare:
300 g (101/2 oz) saltwater fish fillets, skinned and diced
1 tomato, peeled, seeded and diced
1 cup green olives, pitted and chopped
Zest of 1 lemon, grated

Fillets of 1 lemon
1/2 cup fresh coriander, chopped
1 tablespoon argan oil (or olive oil)
Half a fresh red hot pepper, seeded and chopped
Olive oil
Coarse sea salt

The Artichokes:
8 fresh globe artichokes (or 8 frozen artichoke bottoms)
Olive oil
Salt and pepper

To Serve:
Argan oil

1. **Prepare the sauce:** Roast the peppers over an open flame until the skin is charred. Transfer to a plastic bag (to make peeling easier) and allow to cool. Peel the skins and remove membranes and seeds.

2. Purée the peppers with the rest of the ingredients for the sauce in a food processor. Strain through a fine sieve and chill.

3. **Prepare the tartare:** Mix the fish with the tomato, olives, coriander, hot pepper and lemon fillets. Season with salt and argan oil.

4. **Prepare the artichokes:** Preheat the oven to 220°C (425°F).

5. Remove the coarse outer leaves and the thistles, peel with a knife until only the bottoms of the artichokes remain, and put them in a bowl of cold water until needed. If using frozen artichoke bottoms, defrost them.

6. Sprinkle the artichoke bottoms with salt and pepper and bake in the hot oven for 10 minutes.

7. **To serve:** Spoon some sauce into the center of a serving dish. Top with one artichoke bottom, fill it with 2 tablespoons of the fish tartare, sprinkle on a few drops of argan oil and serve.

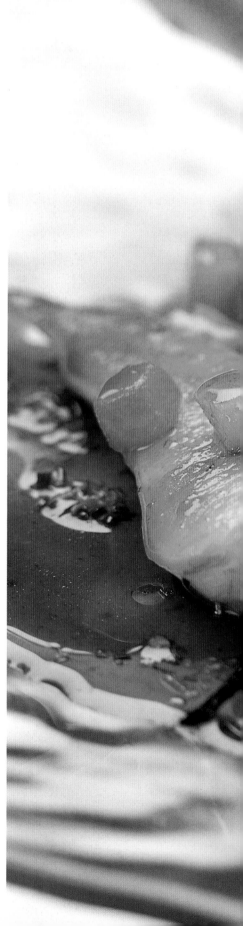

Lamb Shin in Ras-El-Hanoot Spice Mix

Rafi Cohen, Raphael, Tel Aviv

Lamb is the meat of choice to grace the Seder table. The Moroccan spice mixture known as Ras-El-Hanoot (see recipe below) gives this rich and fragrant lamb casserole its unique character.

Ingredients (serves 10)

10 lamb shins, 500 g (about 1 lb) each (have your butcher saw off the top bone)
Salt
Corn starch, for sprinkling
5 tablespoons oil
1 onion, chopped
12 whole cloves garlic, peeled
4 parsley roots, quartered
2 celery roots, quartered
4 carrots, sliced
6 Jerusalem artichokes, peeled and cut into 4 slices each
4 liters (4 quarts) chicken stock or water
2 thyme sprigs
2 bay leaves
2 tablespoons ras-el-hanoot spice mixture

1. Sprinkle corn starch and salt on the lamb. In a wide saucepan, heat the oil and brown the lamb on all sides. Remove and set aside.
2. To the same saucepan, add the onion, garlic, parsley, celery, carrots and Jerusalem artichokes and fry over a high heat for about 5 minutes. Add the stock or water, thyme, bay leaves and ras-el-hanoot spice mixture, stir well and bring to a boil.
3. Return the lamb to the saucepan and bring again to a boil. Lower the heat, cover and cook for 3-4 hours until the meat is very tender. Remove the lid and continue cooking for another 30 minutes until the sauce thickens. Up to this last step the preparation may be done in advance; when ready to finish cooking, remove the lid and cook for 45 minutes.

Raphael's Ras-El-Hanoot

Ras-El-Hanoot ("Top of the Store") is a Moroccan spice mixture for which every spice vender has a secret formula. It is used to season meat.

Ingredients (makes half a cup)

2 tablespoons paprika
2 tablespoons turmeric
1 tablespoon fennel seeds
1 tablespoon aniseed
2 tablespoons dry coriander seeds

Pound all of the ingredients together in a mortar and pestle (or use the bottom of a glass) to a coarse, not fully ground, texture. Keep any unused portion in a tightly closed jar.

Mina del Pesach — Passover Matzo Pie

The custom of Balkan Jews to serve a rich, savory pastry at every important meal led to the creation of mina — the Passover substitute for bourekas with meat. The preparation is similar to that of quiche or pie made with puff or short pastry, with matzos serving as the crust. This pie may be prepared ahead and heated in the oven before serving.

Ingredients (for a 24 cm/12 inch diameter round baking dish)

The Crust:
8-10 matzos
1/2 cup olive oil, for brushing
The Filling:
4 tablespoons oil
2-3 onions, chopped finely
3 cloves garlic
700 g (11/2 lb) ground beef or lamb

Salt and coarsely ground black pepper
1/2 teaspoon cinnamon
4 eggs
2-3 tablespoons matzo meal
1-2 potatoes, cooked and mashed
1/2 cup pine nuts, roasted
1/2 cup fresh parsley, chopped (optional)
3/4 cup chicken stock

1. Dip the matzos in a bowl of cold water for a few seconds, wrap in a towel and leave for 10-15 minutes until they soften and become flexible.
2. **Prepare the filling:** Fry the onions in the oil until they become golden. Add the garlic and the meat and continue frying until the meat is done.
3. Add the spices, remove from the stove, cool slightly and add the eggs, matzo meal, mashed potatoes, pine nuts and parsley. Mix well.
4. Preheat the oven to 180°C (350°F).
5. **Assemble the pie:** Grease the baking dish. Brush the wet matzos on both sides with a little oil and arrange on the bottom, draping enough over the sides to later cover the filling.
6. Spoon half the meat mixture into the baking dish and flatten. Cover with a layer of matzos and top with the remaining half of the meat. Fold the matzo draped over the side of the dish to cover the filling, brush with oil, place an additional matzo on top and brush that too with oil.
7. Bake for 25-30 minutes or until golden. Remove from the oven, spoon the soup over the pie and return to the oven for another 5 minutes.
8. Cool slightly and serve.

Passover "Napoleon" with Coconut Cream

Adi Blumenfeld, Touch Food Cooking School, Raanana

This is the Passover version of the classic French dessert. Caramel-coated matzos is a clever substitute for the puff pastry.

Ingredients (serves 8)

The Coconut Cream:
800 ml (12/3 pints, 2 cans) coconut milk
80 g (3 oz, 5 tablespoons) corn starch
8 egg yolks
150 g (51/2 oz) sugar
3 teaspoons rose water or a few drops rose essence

The Caramel Matzos:
5 matzos
Oil for frying
250 g (9 oz, 11/4 cups) sugar
240 ml (81/2 fl oz, 1 cup) coconut milk

To Serve:
Fresh strawberries, halved lengthwise
Confectioners' sugar

1. **Prepare the coconut cream:** Dissolve the corn starch in 1/2 cup of coconut milk, add the egg yolks and most of the sugar and beat well. Bring the remaining coconut milk with the remaining sugar to a boil and add gradually to the egg mixture. Pour into a pan and heat slowly, stirring constantly, until the cream thickens. Remove from the stove and add the rose water. Cool and transfer to a piping bag.

2. **Prepare the caramel matzos:** Wet each matzo with water, wrap in a kitchen towel and set aside for 30 minutes. Cut the matzos into circles using a ring cutter, or into small squares, and fry in oil on both sides until golden. Remove from the pan and dry on paper towel.

3. Dissolve the sugar in a saucepan with a few tablespoons of water over low heat until a light caramel color. Bring the coconut milk to a boil and gradually pour into the caramel, stirring constantly. Cook for a few minutes until smooth and creamy. Dip the fried matzos in the caramel cream for 2 minutes, remove carefully and cool.

4. **To serve:** Place a matzo disk or square on a serving plate. Pipe some of the cream over it and top with fruit. Cover with another matzo, pipe more cream, top with fruit, and cover with another matzo. Dust with confectioners' sugar and serve.

Flourless Chocolate and Pistachio Cake

Barry Sayag, Tatti Boulangerie, Givatayim

Baking delicious cakes without flour is a challenge. The traditional solution is to use a combination of finely ground nuts and a small amount of matzo meal and/or corn starch. The following cake has no flour substitutes at all, only finely ground almonds and coarsely ground pistachio nuts for added crunch and flavor. Hazelnuts can substitute for pistachios.

Ingredients (for 1 loaf pan)

2 eggs
2 egg yolks
110 g (4 oz, 1/2 cup + 1 tablespoon) sugar
160 g (51/2 oz, 11/2 cups) pistachio nuts, coarsely ground
10 g (1 tablespoon) cocoa powder

80 g (3 oz, 3/4 cup) almonds, finely ground
160 g (51/2 oz, 3/4 cup) chocolate chips
2 egg whites
20 g (3/4 oz, 11/2 tablespoons) melted butter

1. Preheat the oven to 160°C (310°F).
2. Beat the eggs and the egg yolks in a mixer with 80 g (3 oz) of the sugar to a thick and fluffy cream.
3. Add the pistachio nuts, almonds, cocoa powder and chocolate chips and mix to a smooth batter.
4. Beat the 2 egg whites with the remaining sugar to soft peaks and fold in the nut and egg mixture. Stir in the melted butter.
5. Pour the batter into a well-greased pan and bake for about 40 minutes, until a toothpick comes out dry with a few crumbs adhering. Serve at room temperature.

Shavuot

The lovely *bikkurim* ceremony on an Israeli kibbutz is the best place to experience the spirit of Shavuot. A procession of tractors and wagons festooned with flowers and laden with wheat and the first fruits (*bikkurim*) of the harvest are paraded before a cheering crowd, while young parents proudly present their own *bikkurim* — babies born during the past year. Singing and dancing, loads of food and a general mood of merriment prevail. A more modest urban version of this ceremony takes place in schools and kindergartens throughout the country, where children clad in white, wreaths on their heads, carry baskets of fruit and sing traditional Shavuot songs.

Shavuot occurs exactly seven weeks after Passover — from which it gets its name, 'weeks'. It commemorates two events: the custom of bringing offerings to The Temple from among the first fruits of the harvest and the first animals born to the flocks. Hence its other names: Harvest Festival and First Fruits (Bikkurim) Festival. And, it commemorates giving of the Torah to the People of Israel on Mount Sinai.

The holiday is one of the three Pilgrimages to The Temple, the other two being Passover and Sukkot, The Feast of the Tabernacles. Among its many customs are decorating the synagogue with greenery, reciting the Book of Ruth, and staying up all night studying the Bible.

It is interesting that despite this wealth of customs and traditions, if you ask the average Israeli what Shavuot means to him or her, the immediate response would be "cheesecake". Indeed, cheesecakes and other dairy delicacies are the designated Shavuot food. With every passing year the culinary aspect of this early summer festival becomes more pronounced, helped along by the aggressive marketing of the dairy industry. Public opinion polls show time and again that Shavuot is considered the most delicious of local holidays. Apart from cheesecake, there is no specific dairy dish exclusively associated with this holiday, giving amateur cooks and professional chefs free rein to explore new dairy-based recipes. It is in this spirit that we assembled the following collection.

Mediterranean Pashtida (Quiche)

Uri Scheft, Lechamim Bakery, Tel Aviv

Pashtida is a Hebrew word derived from German (*pastete*) and Italian (*pastetta*). It has been used since the Middle Ages for any baked dish based on a batter of eggs and cheese, vegetables, meat, fish, or any combination thereof, with or without a crust. Cheese-based *pashtidas* like this one are a staple of Shavuot.

Ingredients (for two 24 cm/10 inch quiche pans)

The Pastry Shell (Crust):
350 g (121/2 oz, 21/2 cups) flour
1 level teaspoon salt
250 g (9 oz) chilled butter, cut into pieces
70 ml (21/2 fl oz) cold water

The Filling:
1 eggplant, diced
Olive oil for baking
1 onion, halved and sliced thinly
1 leek (white part only), sliced thinly
3 sweet red peppers

1 cup fresh parsley or coriander, chopped
500 g (1 lb 2 oz) feta cheese, diced
20 cherry tomatoes, halved
70 g (21/2 oz) shelled pumpkin seeds

Sauce Royale:
750 ml (11/2 pint, 3 cups) whipping cream
4 eggs
Pinch of nutmeg
Salt and freshly ground black pepper
2 cloves garlic, crushed

1. **Prepare the pastry shell:** Mix the flour and salt in a food processor. Add chilled butter and pulse until the mixture forms crumbs. Add water and pulse only until a ball of smooth dough is formed. Cover with cling wrap and refrigerate for one hour.
2. Roll out a thin layer of dough on a well-floured surface and line the quiche pans. Chill for at least 30 minutes.
3. **Prepare the filling:** Preheat the oven to 200°C (400°F).
4. Roast the peppers over an open flame until the skin is charred. Cool in a sealed plastic bag (to make peeling easier). Peel, remove seeds and membranes and cut into strips.
5. Pour some olive oil over the eggplant and bake for about 20 minutes, until the cubes are light brown and tender. Remove but don't turn the oven off.
6. Sauté the onions and leeks in olive oil until they turn translucent. Remove from the pan and cool.
7. **Prepare the Sauce Royale:** Combine all the ingredients into a smooth mixture.
8. **Assemble and bake:** Spread the onion-leek mixture on the pastry shell, lay on the eggplant cubes and pepper strips, sprinkle the parsley or coriander and carefully pour on the sauce. Arrange the cheese cubes and cherry tomatoes and sprinkle with the pumpkin seeds.
9. Bake for about 25 minutes until golden-brown. If the quiche browns too quickly, cover with aluminum foil and remove the foil 5 minutes before taking the quiche out of the oven.

Bouikous con Kashkaval — Sephardic Cheese Buns

These aromatic buns are truly delectable and so easy to make. The dough may be prepared in advance, wrapped, kept in the refrigerator, and baked just before serving.

Ingredients (makes 30 bite-size buns)

350 g (121/2 oz, 21/2 cups) self-rising flour
250 g (9 oz) *gvina levana* (soft white cheese) or ricotta
200 g (7 oz) hard cheese (gruyere, kashkaval or Parmesan), grated

150 g (5 oz) brinza or feta, crumbled
1 egg
200 g (7 oz) butter, melted
The Coating:
50 g (2 oz) hard cheese, grated

1. Preheat the oven to 200°C (400°F).
2. In a bowl, mix all the ingredients (except the cheese for the coating) into a very soft dough. Add some flour if it's too moist.
3. Divide into 30 balls the size of apricots. Dip the dome of each ball in the grated coating cheese and arrange them evenly spaced on a tray lined with baking paper.
4. Bake for about 20 minutes until the buns are golden. Cool slightly on a rack and serve at once.

Labane — Yogurt Cheese

Sour tasting and creamy, labane is the easiest cheese to make at home. Sheep milk yogurt makes an especially good labane. Cow milk yogurt is also good.

Ingredients

5-6 cups yogurt, preferably sheep milk (at least 3% fat)
2 teaspoons salt
Olive oil

1. Mix the yogurt with the salt and pour into the center of a clean cheesecloth. Tie the corners together to form a sack.
2. Hang the sack over the sink or a bowl and let the liquid drain for 24 hours. Hang over a bowl in the refrigerator for another 24 hours or more until it reaches the desired consistency.
3. Transfer to a jar and cover with olive oil. Seal tightly.
4. **To serve:** Spread on a plate and pour over some olive oil.
5. **To make labane balls:** Prepare thick labane and roll it into 2-3 cm (1 inch) balls. Transfer to a jar and cover completely with olive oil. Seal tightly. No refrigeration is needed as the oil will keep the cheese from spoiling.

Israeli Cheesecake

No Shavuot celebration is complete without a cheesecake. The following is one of the most popular and easy to make. This cake is prepared with *gvina levana*, soft low-fat white cheese, but if unavailable you can use cream cheese.

Ingredients (for a 20×27 cm / 8×11 inch rectangular baking dish)

The Crust and the Topping:
200 g (7 oz, 1 2/3 cups) crumbled petit-beurre cookies
120 g (4 oz) melted butter
25 g (1 oz, 2 tablespoons) sugar
The Filling:
200 g (7 oz) butter

200 g (7 oz, 1 cup) sugar
1 egg
1 egg yolk
250 g (one small container, 9 oz) soft white cheese (*gvina levana*)
200 g (one small container, 7 oz) sour cream

1. **Prepare the crust and the topping:** Combine the crumbled cookies with the sugar and melted butter.
2. Press two-thirds of the mixture onto the bottom of the baking dish. Freeze for 15 minutes until the crust solidifies. Keep the rest for the topping.
3. **Prepare the filling:** Beat the butter with the sugar, egg and egg yolk in a mixer for 10 minutes until creamy and fluffy.
4. Gently fold in the cheese and the sour cream and pour the filling into the prepared crust. Coat with the remaining cookie crumb mixture and refrigerate for 24 hours before serving.

Variation Replace *gvina levana* with an equal amount of cream cheese.

Malabi Mousse Cheesecake

Malabi, a Middle Eastern dairy dessert (p. 98), is the source of inspiration for this beautiful and exotically fragrant cheesecake. Orange blossom water (*zahir* in Arabic) is used to perfume both the mousse and the jelly topping. It is similar to rose water, but the bouquet is more delicate. Rose water can substitute.

Ingredients (for a 26 cm/10 inch diameter springform pan)

1 26 cm/10 inch sponge base
The Malabi Mousse:
14 g (1 sachet , 1/2 oz) gelatin
80 ml (3 fl oz) water
240 ml (81/2 oz, 1 cup) milk
1/2 cup dried rosebuds (available at spice shops and Middle Eastern markets)
5 drops orange blossom water
3 egg whites
50 g (2 oz, 1/4 cup) sugar
500 g (1 lb 2 oz) mascarpone cheese

500 ml (1/2 quart, 2 cups) whipping cream
100 g confectioners' sugar
The Topping:
300 ml (101/2 oz, 11/4 cups) water
100 g (31/2 oz, 1/2 cup) sugar
14 g (1 sachet , 1/2 oz) gelatin
5 drops orange blossom water
150 g (5 oz) frozen or fresh berries
Unsprayed rose petals (optional)

1. **Prepare the mousse:** Pour the water in a bowl and sprinkle on the gelatin.
2. Bring the milk with dried rosebuds to a boil in a small saucepan. Turn off the heat, cover and let stand for 30 minutes. Strain the milk and return to the pan. Bring to a simmer and remove from the stove. Add the softened gelatin and the orange blossom water and cool to room temperature.
3. Beat egg whites in a mixer for 8 minutes, until they hold stiff peaks.
4. Beat the cheese with the confectioners' sugar and whipping cream until smooth and fluffy.
5. Add 2-3 tablespoons of the peaked egg whites to the milk and mix well. Add some more egg whites and mix. Fold the mixture into the remaining egg whites. Gently fold in the cheese mixture.
6. Place the sponge base in the bottom of the springform pan. Pour the mousse over the base and freeze for at least two hours.
7. **Prepare the topping:** Pour water in a bowl and sprinkle over the gelatin to soften.
8. Bring the water and sugar to a boil, remove from the stove and add the softened gelatin and the orange blossom water. Mix well to dissolve the gelatin. Arrange the berries over the frozen cake and pour on the gelatin mixture. Refrigerate until the jelly solidifies, release the cake from the pan, garnish with rose petals and serve.

Ramadan

Ramadan is the ninth month of the Islamic calendar and the holiest month of the Islamic year. The religion commands that all adult believers fast from sunrise to sunset during the entire month.

Paradoxically, the Ramadan fast has given rise to some exquisite culinary customs. Families gather at sunset for a large traditional meal, followed by a selection of delectable sweets. During the evening hours friends and relatives visit back and forth bearing more sweet offerings, from store-bought candy and baklava to homemade sweetmeats.

Eid El-Fitr (the Feast of Breaking the Fast) marks the end of Ramadan and the beginning of a new month. The day starts with communal prayers and continues with elaborate festive meals. Here are some examples of the rich delights that Muslim Arabs in Israel enjoy during the month of Ramadan and the holiday of Eid El-Fitr.

Mansaf

A traditional lamb casserole served at weddings as well as at the Eid El-Fitr feast. The dish is traditionally accompanied by warm yogurt.

Ingredients (serves 6-8)

6 lamb shanks, about 500 g (1 lb) each
1 cup olive oil
1 cup pine nuts
1 cup blanched almonds
1 teaspoon ground cardamom

1 teaspoon baharat spice mix (p. 299)
1 teaspoon turmeric
1 teaspoon salt
1/2 teaspoon freshly ground black pepper
1 kg (2 lb 4 oz) rice

1. Heat olive oil in a wide saucepan and fry the pine nuts until golden. Remove with a slotted spoon and drain on paper towel. Fry the almonds in the same oil and drain them too on paper towel.
2. Add the lamb shanks to the pan and seal on all sides, until the meat turns golden. Remove with a slotted spoon and save the oil.
3. Transfer the meat to a different pan and cover with water. Cook for 3 hours, until it is very tender and almost falls off the bone. Adjust seasoning towards the end of the cooking cycle. Strain and save the cooking liquid. Keep the meat warm.
4. Fry the rice in the saved oil for a few minutes. Add about 1 1/2 liters (1 1/2 quarts) of the cooking liquid, bring to a boil, lower the heat, cover and cook for 20 minutes.
5. To serve: Spread the rice on a large tray or serving dish and arrange the meat on top. Sprinkle with the pine nuts and almonds and serve immediately.

Attayif

These small fluffy pancakes filled with nuts or cheese and doused with syrup are one of the most famous Ramadan delicacies. The pancakes can be bought at pastry shops, where they are made on the premises on a special electric griddle, and stuffed at home.

Ingredients (makes about 35 pancakes)

The Syrup:
2 cups sugar
1 cup water
1 tablespoon lemon juice
1 tablespoon orange blossom water

The Pancakes:
1/2 teaspoon dry yeast
1 teaspoon sugar
280 ml (10 fl oz, 11/4 cups) water
280 g (10 oz, 2 cups) flour
Pinch of salt
Butter for frying

The Cheese Filling:
1 cup ricotta cheese or fresh goat cheese
1/2 teaspoon cinnamon

The Nut filling:
1 cup walnuts or pecans, coarsely chopped
1/4 cup sugar
1 teaspoon cinnamon

Oil for deep-frying
Chopped pistachio nuts for garnish

1. **Prepare the syrup:**   Bring the sugar, water and lemon juice to a boil, reduce the heat and simmer for about 10 minutes. Turn off the heat and add the orange blossom water. Refrigerate.

2. **Prepare the pancakes:** Sprinkle the yeast and sugar over the water and set aside for a few minutes, until the yeast foams. Mix the flour and salt and pour over the yeast mixture. Stir to a smooth batter. Set aside for 2 hours.

3. Heat a small non-stick frying pan or pancake griddle and oil it lightly with butter. Pour 1-2 tablespoons of batter into the pan and fry on medium heat on one side only, until small bubbles appear on the surface. Remove to a platter, and continue frying until all the batter is used up.

4. Mix the ingredients for the two kinds of fillings. Place a heaping tablespoon of cheese or nut filling in the center of the uncooked side of each pancake. Fold over and pinch the edges to make them stick together.

5. Heat the oil for deep-frying and fry the filled pancakes in small batches for 2-3 minutes, until golden brown. Remove with a slotted spoon and drain the excess oil on paper towel.

6. Pour the cold syrup in a deep bowl. Dip the hot pancakes in the cold syrup. Sprinkle with chopped pistachio nuts. Attaif can be served hot or warm.

Baked Attayif Arrange the filled pancakes on a baking sheet, sprinkle with melted butter and bake for 10 minutes at 200°C (400°F). Douse with cold syrup and serve.

Attayif pancakes coming off the griddle —
the sign of Ramadan

Makroud — Date and Sesame Cookies

It takes time and practice to produce these dainty sweetmeats, but the result definitely justifies the effort. The main ingredient is pitted pressed dates, called *ajwa* in Arabic. It is sold in Middle Eastern food stores and markets. If unavailable, pit ordinary dried dates and chop them in a food processor (you may need to add a little bit of oil). Another special ingredient is mahlab, an aromatic spice made from the dried kernel of a small black cherry tree that grows wild in the Mediterranean region. It is frequently used in baking, especially in breads and cookies. Mahlab is not readily available outside the region, though you may find it in a Greek or Middle Eastern food shop. It can be omitted, but it definitely adds a lovely aroma — a combination of rose water and almonds. This recipe comes from the Safadi Family of Nazareth.

Ingredients (makes 70-80 cookies)

The Dough:
500 g (1 lb 2 oz, 3 1/2 cups) flour
15 g (1/2 oz, 1 tablespoon) fresh yeast
240 ml (8 1/2 fl oz, 1 cup) corn oil
120 ml (4 fl oz, 1/2 cup) olive oil
1/2 tablespoon ground aniseed
1/2 tablespoon mahlab (optional)
240 ml (8 1/2 fl oz, 1 cup) lukewarm water

The Filling:
500 g (1 lb 2 oz) pressed pitted dates
60 ml (2 fl oz, 1/4 cup) corn oil
1/2 teaspoon cinnamon
1/4 teaspoon nutmeg
Pinch ground cloves

The Coating:
450 g (1lb) sesame seeds

1. **Prepare the dough:** Crumble the yeast and mix with the flour and spices. Add the two kinds of oil and stir. Add water gradually and knead by hand for 2-3 minutes into a soft, smooth dough. Set aside.
2. **Prepare the filling:** Mix the dates with the oil and spices to a soft malleable paste.
3. Divide the dough into balls the size of a fist. Divide the date filling paste into an identical number of balls. Both the dough and the dates will be dripping with oil.
4. Preheat the oven to 220°C (425°F).
5. Sprinkle a generous amount of sesame seeds on a work surface. Place a ball of dough on the work surface and flatten it with the palm of your hand to make a big flat pita. Put a ball of date filling on top of the dough and sprinkle more sesame seeds. Turn over and roll out to a disk the size of a large serving plate. The sesame seeds will keep the dates from sticking to the surface. Turn over again so the dates are on top and, using your hands, work from the outside to the center, rolling up the dough and filling to form two identical logs side by side. Cut them apart and, using your hands, give each log a rectangular shape.
6. Cut the rectangles into 5 cm (2 inch) cookies and arrange on baking sheets.
7. Bake for 10 minutes until the cookies are golden-brown. Cool slightly and serve, or store up to a month in a sealed jar.

Wine Cellars in Domaine du Castel

Wine Fever in the Holy Land

"*The Land of Israel staggers beneath its burden of history and myth, and much of that intoxicating scripturally sanctified baggage is wine-sodden. What Christian would not like to drink the wine of Cana or Galilee after a thoughtful afternoon amongst the splintery, fissured olives of Gethsemane? What Jew would prefer a French kosher wine to one from the Land from which (according to the Book of Numbers) Moses' spies returned bearing an enormous cluster of grapes suspended from a pole?*"

Andrew Jefford, Evening Standard Wine Guide

Scratch the surface of an Israeli map and you will find a winemaker, making wine with individuality and passion. There are more than 200 wineries, ranging from large commercial operations producing millions of bottles to small domestic ones making a few thousand for friends and family. For the curious tourist and the adventurous wine lover, there is no end to the variety of wineries to visit and wines to taste: from the northern Golan Heights, as high as 1200 meters above sea level, down to the lowest depths of the Negev Desert. There are technologically advanced wineries that would not be out of place in Napa or Barossa, and ones where lack of expertise is compensated for by boundless enthusiasm. There are moshav (cooperative) wineries and kibbutz (collective) wineries. There are wineries run by ultra-orthodox Jews and wineries operated by Christian monks. There is even one called Mony, owned by an Arab family, that makes kosher wine and is situated in a monastery!

Archeological remains of a rich winemaking past abound in the region, dating back at least 2,000 years before the Greeks and Romans took the vine to Europe. The Israelites' interest in winegrowing is a recurring theme in the Bible and the Talmud. Of the seven species with which Eretz Israel was blessed, the vine was first among the fruits.

For Jews there is no communal, religious or family life without wine. A Jewish boy will have his first taste of wine at his circumcision when only eight days old, and the wedding ceremony includes the bride and groom sipping from the same cup of wine. Every Sabbath starts with a blessing over ▷

Carmel's Australian-trained winemaker Sam Soroka

Early 20th Century bottle from Carmel's Archive

◁ wine, the Kiddush, and on Passover four glasses of wine must be drunk during the ritual Seder meal.

Winemaking in the land of Israel was at its peak during the period of The Second Temple. When the Romans destroyed The Temple in 68 CE, the Jews were dispersed and the once proud industry forsaken. It took a Rothschild to renew the tradition. Baron Edmond de Rothschild financed the intensive planting of vineyards throughout the 1880s, and built wineries in the 1890s using expertise from Bordeaux. In 1882, Jewish immigrants from Russia and Romania settled in Rishon Le Zion, south of Tel Aviv, and Zichron Yacov, south of Haifa. On the advice of Rothschild's French experts, they turned to vineyards after the failure of their initial efforts to grow wheat and potatoes.

Whereas his father paid 4 million francs to purchase the famous Bordeaux winery, Chateau Lafite, Edmond de Rothschild invested 11 million francs to create Carmel, Israel's first brand and first exporter. Carmel has managed to make wine without ever missing a harvest — under Ottoman rule, the British Mandate, and finally the State of Israel. Three future Israeli prime ministers — David Ben-Gurion, Levi Eshkol and Ehud Olmert — worked for this historic company, which was also the site of the first telephone and electricity in Israel.

For most of the early years, the main market for Israeli wine was Jewish communities around the world who wanted sacramental wines only from *Eretz Ha'Kodesh*, The Holy Land. The young State of Israel had no wine culture to speak of. Until the 1970s, Israelis preferred Coca-Cola, occasionally sipping a sweet red wine or a white wine spritzer. They eventually graduated to semi-dry wines like Grenache Rosé and Emerald Riesling. Most consumers offered a dry wine would complain it was sour.

The revolution began in 1983 when Golan Heights Winery was founded using vineyards on the Golan. It invited the services of California wine consultant Peter Stern, who brought modern viticulture and winemaking technology to Israel. Its Yarden wines began winning prizes in international competitions and their success continues until today. It showed the world, and more importantly, Israelis, that it was possible to make world-class wines in Israel.

In the 1990s the economy was good, peace was in the air, and Israelis traveling abroad returned hungry for the good things in life. One of the results was an upsurge in food and wine culture. Serious wine shops opened, wine magazines and wine books were published in Hebrew, a number of distributors began importing fine wine from all over the world, and new, small boutique and domestic wineries appeared on the scene. ▷

Whereas his father paid four million francs to purchase the famous Bordeaux winery, Chateau Lafite, Edmond de Rothschild invested 11 million francs to create Carmel, Israel's first brand and first exporter

At the turn of the century a new kind of investor was attracted to the Israeli wine scene: idealists who spared no expense to build wineries, with attention to aesthetics and the determination to produce high quality wines.

his son, Assaf. Restaurateur Eli Ben Zaken taught himself winemaking out of a book. The first wine he made turned out to be pretty good! Serena Sutcliffe, Master of Wine and Head of Sotheby's wine department, tasted the 1992 vintage and remarked it was the best wine she had tasted from Israel. For Eli Ben Zaken, a hobby turned into his livelihood and he built a beautiful winery, Domaine du Castel, in the mountains west of Jerusalem.

Canadian-born Barry Saslove had his own dreams. Enamored with the world of wine, he started giving wine appreciation courses in the 1990s, and later pioneered winemaking courses that were attended by the new wave of boutique winery owners. He now has his own Saslove Winery, which he runs together with his daughter.

The number of new wineries continued to soar and at the turn of the century a new kind of investor was attracted to the Israeli wine scene: idealists who spared no expense to build wineries, with attention to aesthetics and the determination to produce high quality wines. Wineries like Amphorae, Chateau Golan, Clos de Gat and Ella Valley were the result. Instead of aiming for gradual growth from modest beginnings like many of the previous start-ups, these wineries were geared to produce commercial quantities almost immediately.

The large wineries fought back with investments of their own. Golan Heights Winery built a beautiful new facility in the Upper Galilee. Barkan purchased Segal, a winery and importer, and built a large new winery next to the largest vineyard in the country, near Rehovot. Carmel established small state-of-the-art wineries at Ramat Dalton in the Upper Galilee and Tel Arad in the northeast Negev, and renovated the Zichron Yacov Wine Cellars. Efrat, which began as a winery in the Old City of Jerusalem in 1870, moved to new premises and changed their name to Teperberg.

The modern Israeli wine industry was built on French knowledge and made its major advance with California expertise. Today the major influence may well be Australian. Most leading wineries have state-of-the-art equipment and employ internationally trained winemakers.

Whereas Israel once had to import its wine expertise, now young Israelis are attracted to a career in wine like bees to honey. Countless numbers study in wine schools in

◁ Some of them began with veteran vineyard owners who decided to become winemakers. Yonatan Tishbi's grandfather was one of the settlers who planted the original Rothschild vineyards, but a hundred years later, after a visit to Italy, Yonatan decided to make and sell his own wine instead of selling grapes. He founded Tishbi Winery, which is still a family operation. Ronnie James was another grower-turned-winemaker: after thirty years of tending the vineyards of Kibbutz Tzora, he founded the first kibbutz winery in the country in the hills ascending to Jerusalem.

Other boutique winemakers began as hobbyists. One of the first was chemistry professor Yair Margalit, who became attracted to winemaking and in 1989 started what was to become the first serious boutique winery in the country. He acted as a catalyst, advising other new boutique wineries, and wrote technical books on winemaking that are read all over the world. He is now an elder statesman of Israeli winemaking and has been joined in the family business by

▷

Yair Margalit, founder of the first
serious boutique winery in Israel

The bottling line at Golan Heights Winery

California, Australia, France and Italy. The wine industry benefits from the agricultural know-how and technology for which Israel is known. Drip-feed irrigation that transformed farming worldwide is an Israeli invention. Meteorological stations in the vineyards of the Golan and vineyards planted in the Negev Desert using brackish water show that Israel's viticulturists are able to make the most of the vastly differing conditions in the various grape-growing regions.

Eager for Israel to produce fine wine, Baron Rothschild initially planted the main Bordeaux varieties of grapes in the 1880s: Cabernet Sauvignon, Cabernet Franc and Malbec. But when the vineyards were destroyed by phylloxera, they were replanted with varieties from the south of France, like Carignan, which was the workhorse grape of Israeli wine until the early 1990s. Part of the quality revolution in the past twenty years has entailed going back to planting the classic international varieties. The main varieties grown today are Cabernet Sauvignon, Merlot, Chardonnay and Sauvignon Blanc. Other well-known varieties like Cabernet Franc and Gewurztraminer are yielding wines meeting international standards. Still others are being experimented with in different regions as Israel strives to find the correct varieties for its terroir.

Some of Israel's red wines, in particular the Cabernet Sauvignons and Bordeaux-style blends, are truly world-class. They exhibit a great depth of color, and are very fruit forward with fine structure and complexity. They are arguably better than the whites, although good Sauvignon Blancs are being produced. Apart from its red wines, Israel has also won major awards for traditional method sparkling wine and some luscious, high-quality dessert wines. Many believe that Syrah/Shiraz will eventually be the best variety of all, being well suited to Israel's Mediterranean climate.

In spite of its compact dimensions, Israel has a wide range of microclimates. The cooler vineyards at the higher altitudes of the Upper Galilee, Golan Heights and Judean Hills have proved to yield the highest quality wines. The Golan Heights in the northeast is a volcanic plateau rising from the Sea of Galilee to snow-covered Mount Hermon. The central and northern Golan, rising 1200 meters above sea level, has the finest vineyards. Golan Heights Winery in the town of Katzrin is the dominant winery here — indeed in the whole country — thanks to its use of the latest technology and a relentless dedication to quality.

The Galilee is a new wine region, with vineyards planted relatively recently. The Lower Galilee has its share of vineyards, but those in the Upper Galilee are in greatest demand. The main vineyard areas are the Kedesh Valley

Eli Ben Zaken in the vineyards of Domaine du Castel

on the Lebanese border and Merom HaGalil near Mount Meron. Many of Israel's finest wineries, even if not situated in the vicinity, produce their best wines from grapes grown in the Upper Galilee. This beautiful area of forests, rising peaks and stony ridges, the Provence of Israel, is the country's most scenic wine region. One of the best local wineries is Galil Mountain, situated at Yiron, whose meticulously made wines come from five nearby vineyards.

The valleys of Mount Carmel around the winery towns of Zichron Yacov and Binyamina, where cool breezes blow off

Some of Israel's red wines, in particular the Cabernet Sauvignons and Bordeaux-style blends, are truly world-class. They exhibit a great depth of color, and are very fruit forward with fine structure and complexity.

◁ the Mediterranean, have a large concentration of vineyards planted in Rothschild's time. One short trip will bring you to wineries founded in the 1890s (Carmel), 1950s (Binyamina), 1980s (Tishbi) and the year 2000 (Amphorae), all in close proximity to each other. Carmel's Zichron Yacov Wine Cellars are located here. The rejuvenation of Carmel reflects the dramatic upswing in Israeli wine — a journey from sacramental to single vineyard wines.

The Judean Plain southeast of Tel Aviv is home to Barkan, Israel's second largest winery. They built a magnificent new facility adjacent to the country's largest vineyard and have other extensive ones nearby. Their Barkan and Segal wines represent good value at every price point.

On the way to Jerusalem the plain gives way to the rolling Judean hills, which have become the fastest growing venue for new vineyards and wineries. One of the most interesting wineries in this area is Clos de Gat, an estate winery producing only from its own vineyards. The stone winery building was used as Yitzhak Rabin's headquarters during the 1948 War of Independence. *Gat* is Hebrew for wine press, and sure enough one can be found nestling among the vines. In the center of the Judean Hills that run down the spine of the country lies Castel, a family enterprise that is of immense interest to connoisseurs the world over. Owner and winemaker Eli Ben Zaken produces wines of elegance and finesse that show a pronounced French influence.

The final region of note is the Negev Desert in the south. In the semi-arid, northeast Negev, next to 3000-year-old Tel Arad, lies Yatir Winery. Its vineyards, at 900 meters above sea level, lie within Yatir Forest, Israel's largest forest, planted in 1964. One of the best of the new wave of quality wineries, Yatir has already won a host of medals in both Bordeaux and Israel. Deeper in the dry arid desert are vineyards at Mitzpe Ramon, and at Sde Boker where David Ben-Gurion, Israel's first prime minister, spent his final years. The impressive patches of green vineyards surrounded by sandy rocky desert illustrate how Israel has fulfilled Ben-Gurion's dream of making the desert bloom.

Despite the wine fever of recent years, Israel still remains one of the smallest wine-producing countries. Eight wineries — Carmel, Barkan, Golan Heights, Teperberg, Binyamina,

Top: Victor Schonefield, chief winemaker at Golan Heights Winery. Bottom: Yonatan and Golan Tishbi of Tishbi Winery

Tishbi, Galil Mountain and Dalton — share 90% of the domestic market and are the main exporters. According to famous wine critic Hugh Johnson's Pocket Wine Book, the finest quality Israeli wineries are: Castel and Golan Heights, followed by Yatir, Flam, Margalit, Carmel, Galil Mountain and Clos de Gat, but this is changing year by year as more and more wineries strive for quality.

Israel arguably produces the highest quality wine in the Eastern Mediterranean, the region that gave wine culture to the world. Today Israel has a vibrant, quality-driven wine industry that often surprises conservative wine lovers and connoisseurs in the traditional wine-producing countries. Repeated gold medals and praise by wine critics attest to the quality of Israeli wine. A new "New World" wine country set in one of oldest wine-producing regions on earth.

Special Ingredients

The following foodstuffs are among the most frequently used in local cooking. Not so long ago many of them were quite hard to come by outside Israel or the Middle East, but with globalization, culinary trends and the proliferation of ethnic stores, most are readily available worldwide. If you don't find what you're looking for in a supermarket or gourmet shop, try a Middle Eastern grocer or an on-line store.

Brinza Locally called *gvina melucha* ("salty cheese") or *gvina bulgarit* ("Bulgarian cheese)", it is popular throughout the Balkans. This semi-hard sheep milk cheese cured in brine comes in creamy or crumbly form with a fat content ranging from 5%-16%. Brinza is used in salads and sandwiches as well as baking, notably in preparing fillings for bourekas and quiches. If unavailable Greek feta can substitute.

Bulgur Wheat (Bulgar, Bulghur, Burghul) Parboiled, dried, de-branned cracked wheat grain that is popular in Middle Eastern and Mediterranean cuisines. It is used as a base for stuffed vegetables, and as a primary ingredient in tabuleh (p. 53) and kubbe (p. 115).

Cardamom (Cardamon) The seeds (pods) of the plant Elettaria cardamomum in crushed or ground form, used as an aromatic spice in rice and meat dishes, in Arab-style coffee, and as an ingredient of Middle Eastern spice mixtures like baharat and hawaij. The flavor of cardamom seeds deteriorates after grinding, so whole pods should be crushed just before use and not stored for long periods of time. The flavor and aroma of green pods are superior to those of bleached ones.

Coriander (Cilantro) Without doubt the most important fresh herb in Middle Eastern cooking, used fresh in salads and dips, and added to rice, meat and chicken as well as soups.

Couscous (Maftoul) A North African specialty made of processed and steamed semolina. The name refers to the ingredient as well as to the dish. Preparing couscous the traditional way is a time-consuming process. Fortunately, instant, pre-steamed couscous is readily available, and closely resembles the real thing (tips for making the most of instant couscous appear on p. 116). Products labeled "Israeli Couscous" are, in fact, baked pasta (see more on p. 126).

Gvina Levana Literally "white cheese", this soft, fresh creamy cheese is made from cow's milk. It is similar to German Quark. Read more about it on p. 218.

Halva This ultra-sweet Middle Eastern confection is made from ground sesame seeds (just like tahini) sweetened with honey. It is usually sold in slabs or bars, often studded with dried fruit and pistachio nuts, but is also available in strands and as a spread. These last two forms are especially handy for baking and desserts.

Hummus The name refers to chickpeas, the dried fruit of the plant Cicer arietinum, as well as to the dish known in Arabic as *hummus bitahina* (hummus with tahini). Smaller chickpeas, locally called *das*, are the best for hummus spread (p. 47). Larger ones are used for cooking and for falafel (page 68).

Kashkaval Hard sheep milk cheese with a smooth surface and a nutty tangy flavor. The name is derived from Italian Caciocavallo, a Provolone type cheese, but the cheese itself is a typical Balkan staple used extensively in baking and cooking. As it ages it becomes harder and suitable for grating. Greek Kasseri or Italian Pecorino, Provolone or Parmesan are substitutes. In fact, before real Italian Parmesan became available on the local market, Israeli chefs and cookbook writers recommended Kashkaval for grating on pasta.

Labane Soft, white, tangy cheese made from sheep and goat milk yogurt. It is sold in paste form or as little balls immersed in olive oil, and is usually served with olive oil and za'atar. See recipe for homemade labane on p. 269.

Matzo Meal A commercially available product made by grinding matzos into coarse, medium or fine flour. It is used as a substitute for regular wheat flour during the Passover holiday and as an ingredient in matzo balls, gefilte fish and matzo brei.

Mint There are over 20 varieties of mint, but the two most popular in cooking are spearmint and peppermint (the first has a more pungent taste). Both are used in salads and dips, fish and meat (especially lamb) dishes, as well as in sweets. Black tea is often served with fresh mint leaves. ▷

◁ **Orange Blossom Water (*Me Zahir*)** Made from the essential oils of orange blossoms in a distilled water base, it adds fragrance to meat dishes (notably lamb) and desserts.

Phyllo (Filo) Dough (Sheets, Pastry) Paper-thin sheets of dough made from flour and water and very popular in Middle Eastern baking — both sweet and savory. They are sold frozen and must be thawed in the refrigerator before use. As the dough contains no fat, the sheets are brushed with butter or oil before baking.

Pickled Lemons (Moroccan Lemons) A staple of Moroccan cuisine, it adds a unique, strong pickled flavor to lamb, rice and vegetable dishes baked in the traditional tajin, and to fish and meat stews, roasts and grilled meats (recipe on p. 296).

Pine Nuts Some 20 different species of pine produce edible seeds that have been used in Mediterranean and Middle Eastern cooking for thousands of years. They are used in various meat, fish, rice and vegetable dishes as well as in salads, chocolates and desserts. In local cooking they are often mixed with ground lamb meat, added to stuffed vegetables, or sprinkled on hummus and eggplant salad.

Pomegranate Juice and Concentrate Freshly squeezed pomegranate juice has always been a popular drink in the Middle East. Pomegranate concentrate is used mainly in sauces, especially for stuffed vegetables. In modern Israeli cuisine it is also used in salad dressings and desserts. The health benefits of pomegranate and pomegranate products have propelled them to unprecedented popularity in recent years. Pomegranate concentrate, once an exotic ingredient, is now sold in supermarkets and health food stores.

Rose Water and Rose Essence This is the liquid by-product from the distillation of rose petals for the perfume industry. It is used extensively in Middle Eastern cuisine, mainly in the preparation of sweets and desserts. Rose essence is much more concentrated than rose water and therefore should be used more sparingly.

Sesame Seeds The roasted seeds of the sesame plant (Sesamum indicum) have multiple uses. They are sprinkled on breads, bagels, buns and other pastry items; added for extra crunch to salads; included in recipes for sweets; as an ingredient of the za'atar spice mix; and in the dough of crackers and sweetmeats. Tahini and halva are made from ground sesame seeds.

Silan (Date Honey) A very thick sweet syrup made from dried dates, similar to honey but darker in color and with a pronounced caramel taste. It is used as a color and flavor enhancer in slow-cooking dishes like hamin, or in any recipe calling for honey, caramel, molasses or syrup. If unavailable, it can be substituted by honey. Historians believe that the "honey" in the "Land of Milk and Honey" is actually silan.

Sumac (Sumach, Summaq) A violet-red sour spice made from the berries of the wild bush Rhus coriaria and used in Middle Eastern cooking. Sumac picks up any fresh vegetable salad (notably Arab-style salads), and is used to season meat, fish, rice and vegetable dishes.

Tahini (Tahina) A wholesome and highly nutritious paste made from ground sesame seeds. It is an essential ingredient of hummus and the main ingredient in halva. It is extremely popular in local cooking.

Spice Mixes and Condiments

The following products can be found at Jewish and Middle Eastern food shops and on-line stores. Most of them are easy to prepare at home (see recipes on pp. 296-299)

Amba (Bahar of Amba) A thick, amber-colored liquid condiment, similar to chutney, made from pickled mangos and ground fenugreek seeds. Its origin is Southern India but it is particularly popular in Iraqi Jewish cuisine. It has a strong, pungent flavor. Amba is commonly used as a condiment with such popular street foods as shawarma and falafel, as well as in vegetable salads. It is available as a powder in Middle Eastern and Indian grocers and Jewish food markets. It should be mixed with water before use.

Baharat Arabic for "spices", it is the generic name for a mixture of powdered spices but refers mainly to a mix used in Lebanese, Syrian and Iraqi cuisines. Baharat usually contains black pepper, paprika, cumin, coriander, cloves, nutmeg, cinnamon and cardamom. It is used to season meat, fish, rice, vegetable and legume dishes (recipe on p. 299).

Chermula (Shaarmula) A Moroccan seasoning paste usually made from all, or a combination, of hot peppers, garlic, onions, olive oil, lemon juice, cumin, coriander seeds, ginger, paprika, fresh parsley or fresh basil and black pepper. Chermula is used as a sauce mainly for fish dishes and in dressings for salads and legumes.

Filfel Chuma Literally "pepper and garlic" in Arabic, this is the typical hot sauce of Libyan Jewish cuisine. Very similar to Tunisian harissa, it serves as a condiment and as an ingredient in dishes ranging from salads to meat and fish, legumes and rice, and egg preparations like shakshuka (p. 78). Filfel chuma is made from dried sweet and hot peppers, garlic, ground caraway seeds, cumin, lemon juice and salt. It can be prepared at home quite easily (recipe on p. 296).

Harissa Another hot sauce from North African cuisine, similar to filfel chuma and not as hot as Yemenite zhug. It may be eaten as is, spread on a slice of freshly baked bread, but is used extensively as a condiment and as an ingredient in salad dressings and sauces for meat, fish, rice and legume dishes. Harissa is made from dried sweet and hot peppers, garlic, cumin, lemon juice and olive oil. Some versions contain tomatoes, caraway, coriander, and even rose essence. Harissa is sold in cans, tubes and jars, but may be prepared at home quite easily (see recipe on p. 298).

Hawaij There are two completely different Hawaij spice mixtures, both hailing from Yemenite cuisine: one for soup and one for coffee. The soup mixture is used also in stews, curry-style dishes, rice and vegetable dishes, and even as a barbecue rub. Basically, it consists of cumin, black pepper, turmeric and cardamom. More elaborate versions may also contain cloves, caraway, nutmeg, saffron, coriander and ground dried onions. The coffee mixture is completely different and contains aniseed, fennel seeds, ginger and cardamom. It is primarily used in brewing coffee, but also in desserts and cakes and in slow-cooked meat dishes. (Recipe for soup mix on p. 299.)

Ras El-Hanoot (Ras El-Hanout) Arabic for "head of the shop", every spice specialist has a secret formula for this mixture of Moroccan origin. It is used to season various dishes such as couscous, ragout, merguez sausages, stews, fish, grilled meats and hummus (see a sample recipe on p. 256).

Za'atar spice mix Za'atar (Arabic for hyssop) is a Middle Eastern spice mixture based on wild oregano (origanum syriacum or majorana syriace), a plant similar to hyssop (Biblical *eizov*). It also contains salt, sesame seeds, and sometimes cumin and fennel seeds. Wild oregano, also known as white oregano or Lebanese oregano, is a rare protected plant and commercial za'atar often substitutes it with hyssop, oregano or thyme, or a combination of the three. Za'atar is sprinkled on hummus, labane and vegetable salads and used in marinades for fish and chicken. It is also a dry dip with Jerusalem bagel (see recipe for za'atar mix on p. 299).

Zhug A fiery Yemenite condiment made from hot peppers, fresh coriander, garlic and spices. Courageous ones eat zhug as is, spread on bread, or mix it with practically any dish. It is used in the tomato sauce that accompanies Yemenite pastry specialties and to season soups, meat, poultry, fish, rice, legumes and vegetable dishes (recipe on p. 298).

Basic Recipes

Pickled (Moroccan) Lemons

A wonderfully versatile addition to your kitchen pantry: for sandwiches, salads and marinades.

Ingredients

1 kg (2 lb 4 oz) yellow-skinned lemons, sliced thinly or cut into small wedges, pips removed
Coarse salt
5 cloves garlic
2 small hot peppers, red or green

4-6 allspice berries
4 bay leaves
Sweet and/or hot paprika
Freshly squeezed lemon juice, to cover
Oil, to seal

1. Dip the lemon slices/wedges in the coarse salt and arrange them in layers in a sterilized glass jar. Place garlic cloves, whole peppers, bay leaves and allspice berries between the layers of lemon. Press down hard until juice begins to run out and pour the lemon juice on top. To seal, pour a generous layer of oil on top of everything.
2. Close the lid and keep in the refrigerator for 3 months. When the curing process has been completed, discard the garlic, allspice, peppers and bay leaves.

Pickled Lemon Spread Purée the pickled lemons in a food processor to a smooth paste, transfer to sterilized jars and seal with olive oil. This spread will keep refrigerated for many months.

Filfel Chuma

This is the hot condiment of Libyan Jews, originally prepared from dried sweet and hot peppers. This recipe offers a significant shortcut, provided you can obtain top quality cayenne pepper.

Ingredients (makes 1 cup)

10 cloves garlic, minced
1 teaspoon high quality hot paprika (cayenne pepper)
4 tablespoons high quality sweet paprika
1 level teaspoon ground caraway

1 level teaspoon ground cumin
1/2 cup oil, plus more oil, to cover
2 tablespoons freshly squeezed lemon juice
1 teaspoon salt

Mix the ingredients into a smooth paste. Taste and adjust the seasoning. Transfer to a sterilized jar, cover with two tablespoons of oil to prevent spoilage, and store in the refrigerator. It keeps for a long time.

Zhug

No Yemenite Jew will sit down at the table unless a jar of this fiery condiment is present. Veteran Yemenite cooks still prepare zhug using two stones: a large one that serves as a work surface and a smaller one for crushing the ingredients. A mortar and pestle (stone, not copper) are the best alternative but a food processor can also be used.

Ingredients (makes 1 cup)

The Dip:
Cloves from 2 heads of garlic, peeled
1/2 cup hot red peppers
2 cups fresh coriander
1 tablespoon salt
Juice of 1/2 lemon

The Spice Mix:
10 cardamom seeds
10 cloves garlic
1 tablespoon black peppercorns
1 tablespoon cumin seeds

1. Crush the garlic, peppers and coriander to a nearly smooth paste.
2. Lightly roast the spices in a dry skillet. When they cool down grind them in a spice (or coffee) grinder or pulse in a food processor.
3. Mix the dip and the spices and season with salt. Transfer to a jar and pour the lemon juice on top to preserve the green color. Store in the refrigerator.

Harissa

Fairly piquant but nowhere near as hot as zhug, this condiment is a great enhancer of any sandwich and many kinds of salads.

Ingredients (makes 2 cups)

1/2 kg (1 lb 2 oz) dried sweet red peppers
2-3 dried hot red peppers
10 cloves garlic

1/2 cup olive oil
1 tablespoon salt
1 tablespoon ground cumin
Juice of 2 lemons

1. Grind the dried peppers and the garlic with a mortar and pestle or in a meat grinder. A blender may be used as well, but will produce a more liquid harissa.
2. Stir in the olive oil, salt, cumin and lemon juice. Taste and adjust the seasoning.

Variation Add some fresh parsley or fresh coriander while grinding the peppers and garlic.

Za'atar Spice Mix

2 tablespoons sesame seeds
1 tablespoon sumac
1/2 cup dried hyssop or oregano
1/2 teaspoon salt

1. Roast the sesame seeds in a dry skillet until golden.
2. Grind the dried hyssop or oregano with a mortar and pestle or in a food processor.
Mix with the sesame and sumac and season with salt. Keep in an airtight jar.

Za'atar Spread Add 2/3 cup olive oil and grated rind and juice of one lemon.

Baharat Spice Mix

It is best to use whole spices and roast and grind them prior to mixing, but quality ground spices can be used as well.

1 tablespoon ground cardamom
1 tablespoon ground black pepper
1/2 tablespoon ground allspice
1 tablespoon ground cinnamon
1 tablespoon ground dry ginger
1/2 tablespoon ground nutmeg

Mix all the ingredients and keep in an airtight jar.

Hawaij Spice Mix for Soup

1 tablespoon ground black pepper
1 tablespoon ground cumin
1/2 tablespoon ground cardamom
1/2 tablespoon ground caraway
3/4 tablespoon ground turmeric
1/2 tablespoon ground coriander seeds
1/2 teaspoon ground cloves
1/2 tablespoon ground dried coriander leaves

Mix all the ingredients and keep in an airtight jar.

Recipe Index

List of Recipes by ABC